Unit 20

Data Processing

Study Pack

Foundation (NVQ Level 2)

Published August 1995 by Financial Training, 136–142 Bramley Road, London W10 6SR

ISBN 1 85179 637 1

All business entities referred to in this publication are fictitious. Any resemblance to any actual organisation, past or present, is purely coincidental.

Printed by Communications in Print plc, Basildon, Essex.

Contents

Introduction

PREFACE

The assessment guidance given within this Study Pack is in line with the guidance issued by the AAT. You are advised to confirm the methods of assessment to be used for each unit by drawing up an *Assessment plan* with your Approved Assessment Centre (AAC).

Examples of assessment plans are only suggested formats. Other documents or planning methods are equally valid.

INTRODUCTION TO THE EDUCATION AND TRAINING SCHEME

Background to the scheme

The Association of Accounting Technicians (AAT) was founded in 1980 to provide a recognised qualification and membership body for accounting support staff. In 1991 it became the first and only professional accountancy body to adopt competence-led assessment. Each stage of the AAT's new Education and Training Scheme is graded as a National Vocational Qualification (NVQ) or, in Scotland, as a Scottish Vocational Qualification (SVQ) with levels 2 to 4. This means that, once you have completed each stage, you hold a nationally recognised qualification, which is recognised by employers. The scheme is open to anyone, regardless of previous experience or qualifications.

As well as being part of the AAT's membership process, the Education and Training Scheme offers a flexible opportunity for individuals to improve and gain recognition for their skills. In entering the scheme, you do not have to commit yourself to achieving AAT membership; in fact, each successfully completed stage is recognised with the issue of a separate certificate. The AAT will also issue (for an additional fee) certificates to record the successful completion of single or selected units.

If you decide to aim for membership, there are three requirements:

- proven competence
- a minimum period of relevant work experience (usually one year full-time or the part-time equivalent)
- evidence of suitability for membership and commitment to the AAT

This Study Pack deals exclusively with the requirement to prove competence. Further details of the other requirements are available direct from AAT.

Standards

Your aim is to prove your competence against a nationally agreed set of standards. These have been drawn up to reflect the skills, knowledge and understanding required by an accounting technician. They have been prepared to reflect the general types of skills required by any accounting technician rather than any specific job or industry, although some specialisation is possible at the Technician stage (NVQ/SVQ Level 4). You may specialise in accounting practice, industry and commerce or public sector. In addition, if you choose the public sector route, you may specialise in central government, local government or the NHS.

The AAT has decided that the key purpose of an accounting technician is:

To operate, maintain and improve systems to record, plan, monitor and report on the financial activities of an organisation

This key purpose is then broken down into key roles. These are the general areas in which an accounting technician should be competent:

- recording financial transactions
- preparing accounts
- reporting on organisational activities
- contributing to planning and controlling activities
- managing accounting systems
- contributing to assuring the quality of accounting systems
- establishing taxation liabilities
- processing accounting information by computer
- maintaining good office practice

Each role is sub-divided into *units of competence* which identify more specific areas of required competence. These units are arranged into three *stages* which are designed to show you what could normally be expected of accounting technicians as they progress and gain experience. It is important to realise that the stages are guidelines, but we will come back to this later (see *Flexibility* below). Each stage has a name (given by the AAT) and an NVQ/SVQ level. The units for Foundation stage (NVQ/SVQ Level 2) are as follows:

Recording financial transactions

1 Recording and accounting for cash transactions
2 Recording and accounting for credit transactions
3 Recording payroll transactions

Processing accounting information by computer

20 Data processing

Maintaining good office practice

24 Communicating for accounting
25 Monitor and maintain a healthy, safe and secure workplace
26 Create and maintain effective working relationships
27 Store, retrieve and supply information
28 Contribute to the effectiveness of the work flow

The arrangement of the units into stages gives the scheme structure and reflects typical patterns of development and progression. The scheme assumes that, if you are at the Foundation stage, an employer would expect you to be competent in a broad range of complex, technical or professional work activities, performed in a wide variety of contexts. Some of the activities could be complex or non-routine, and there could be some individual responsibility. Working with others – as part of a team, for example – might also be required.

Each unit is in turn divided into elements which are the specific activities within that particular area. Let us now look at one of the elements. You will now need to refer to Unit 20 Element 1 of your *Foundation Student Record Book*. (**Note:** If you have not already registered with the AAT, you should do so as soon as possible. In fact this is vital otherwise you cannot sit any assessments until you have done so. In return they will send you a Student Record Book. You need this book to record your progress.)

Unit 20 Element 1 is a typical element within the standards.

At the top of the page you see the Unit number (in this case 20) followed by a list of *all* the elements for this unit (of which there are three).

The *performance criteria* given for this unit are essentially the things you must get right to be considered competent and are therefore very 'practical'. They also tend to be expressed in very general terms. Remember that the standards are trying to identify general skills rather than skills associated with a particular job or industry.

The *range statement* describes the range of situations in which you have to be able to carry out the performance criteria. The range statement essentially gives more detail, defines terms and gives examples as required.

In this case, the range statement defines *information, computer systems* and *types of inputting*. It also gives examples of databases and unique reference codes.

Assessment

To establish your competence against the standards, you will be assessed by two methods:

- devolved assessment
- central assessment

The AAT decides which units are tested by devolved assessment and which by central assessment, although about half of the units in the whole scheme are tested by both.

Devolved assessment is carried out by an *Approved Assessment Centre* (approved by AAT). Subject to the arrangements of the AAC, devolved assessment is available at any time during the year. The central assessment is set by the AAT itself. It is only offered twice a year (on specified dates in June and December). We will look at the differences between the two types of assessment below. First of all let us look at the methods of assessment for the each unit of the Foundation stage. To complete the Foundation stage, you must gain a credit for *all of the units for your chosen route*.

Foundation	*Devolved assessment*	*Central assessment*
Unit 1 *Recording and accounting for cash transactions*	•	•
Unit 2 *Recording and accounting for credit transactions*	•	
Unit 3 *Recording payroll transactions*	•	
Unit 20 *Data processing*	•	
Unit 24–28 *Office practice*	•	

At this stage, all units are assessed by devolved assessment. In addition, Units 1 and 2 are also assessed by central assessment.

Note: To achieve a credit in a particular unit, you must be assessed as competent in both the devolved assessment and (if applicable) the central assessment. There is no weighting between the two types of assessment; you must be assessed as competent in both to achieve a credit.

Flexibility

Before looking at assessment in more detail, you should be aware of the flexibility allowed by the AAT within the scheme.

You choose the units you attempt

At any one time, you may attempt a complete stage, individual units or a group of units (not necessarily all taken from the same stage).

For example, the following combinations of units would all be valid:

- complete Foundation stage
- Unit 3 *Recording payroll transactions* and Unit 24 *Communicating for accounting*
- a combination of units from both the Foundation and Intermediate stages (units relating to recording financial transactions)

You can attempt the devolved and central assessments when it suits you

Subject to the arrangements agreed with your AAC, you may sit the devolved assessments to fit in with your own progress. You may sit the central assessments in any order and in any combination at any sitting. In fact, the central assessment timetable is arranged to make this possible.

In addition, you do not have to have attempted or passed the devolved assessment for a particular unit before attempting the related central assessment.

There are no time limits

There are no time limits to any part of the scheme and any devolved or central assessment passes are held indefinitely.

Devolved and central assessments

The main differences between the two methods of assessment can be summarised as follows:

	Devolved assessment	*Central assessment*
Assessment carried out by	Approved Assessment Centre (AAC)	AAT
Available	At any time during the year (subject to AAC's arrangements)	June and December only
Covers	All the performance criteria across the entire range statement and some aspects of knowledge and understanding	Selected aspects of knowledge and understanding and performance criteria
Methods of assessment	A variety of flexible methods, including accounting portfolios and projects	Using the same method (ie. written papers set and marked by the AAT)

PLANNING FOR DEVOLVED ASSESSMENT

Your objective

Remember that your objective at all times is to provide the assessor with evidence that you are competent in the performance criteria and have the necessary knowledge and understanding required for each unit. The assessment process is a method of collecting that evidence.

The devolved assessment must test all of the performance criteria across the whole of the range statement. It may also test parts of the knowledge and understanding. Since it concentrates mostly on the performance criteria, the devolved assessment tends to concentrate more on the practical aspects of the activities covered.

Devolved assessment is a very flexible form of assessment, although the AAT suggests the following two main methods at the Foundation stage:

- accounting portfolio
- project work

Unit 20 *Data processing* can be assessed by *accounting portfolio* which is a collection of evidence that you put together to prove that you are competent in the unit. Ideally, this would consist of examples of relevant tasks you have carried out as part of your work or work placement period.

If you have previous experience of the areas being assessed, either through work or by successfully completing another qualification, you may be able to include this evidence in your accounting portfolio. This process is known as *accreditation of prior learning*. We will look at this in more detail below.

The best source of evidence within your accounting portfolio would be *workplace evidence*, whether it arises from *prior learning* or from work which you undertake in the future. We will look at how you can identify workplace evidence below.

If you are unable to submit workplace evidence for some or all of the performance criteria for a particular element, then you may submit other types of evidence. This might include carrying out assignments which could then be included in your accounting portfolio.

In addition to submitting your accounting portfolio, your AAC will probably ask you additional questions which will also form part of the evidence for assessment.

Identifying prior learning

Your first task is to identify areas in which you have prior learning or experience.

You should use the following tables to identify the performance criteria in which you feel you could already demonstrate competence without further study, either because you have already completed another accounting or business studies qualification, or because you have previous or current work experience in these areas.

These tables list the performance criteria and range statements for each of the elements of Unit 20. You should complete the *Prior learning and experience* column with brief details of your specific experience. You should then record in the next column whether this experience is current or past. If your experience arises from another qualification, you should give the year of completion.

Note: Please note that completing this document is only part of the actual assessment process. You will still be required to prepare and submit an accounting portfolio.

Assessment plan for Unit 20: Data processing

Element 1: Input information from source documents into a computer system

Performance criteria	*Prior learning and experience*	*Timing*	*Assessment methods*		*Portfolio Ref.*
			APL	*Other*	
(a) All vital fields are complete.					
(b) Incomplete or unauthorised source documents are referred for clarification.					
(c) All errors in inputting and coding are identified and corrected.					
(d) Correct part of the computer system is used for inputting.					
(e) New unique reference codes are generated as necessary.					
(f) Inputting is completed to agreed deadline.					
(g) Organisational procedures for filing source documents are followed.					
(h) Risks to the information technology environment are minimised at all times.					
Range statement					
• Information: words, numbers, information to be coded using reference codes					
• Source documents: complete and incomplete					
• Computer systems: databases, spreadsheets					

		Timing	*Assessment methods*		*Portfolio Ref.*
Range statement	*Prior learning and experience*		*APL*	*Other*	
• Types of inputting: addition of new information, some of which require the generation of unique reference codes, modification of existing information, deletion/cancelling of existing information					
• Examples of databases: stock control databases, customer databases, sales ledgers, purchase/bought ledgers, employee database and cash logs					
• Examples of unique reference codes: stock codes, customer references, invoice numbers, employee numbers					

Assessment plan for Unit 20: Data processing

Element 2: Locate and retrieve recorded details of requested items from a computer system

Performance criteria	*Prior learning and experience*	*Timing*	*Assessment methods* APL	*Assessment methods* Other	*Portfolio Ref.*
(a) Correct details are retrieved.					
(b) Search facilities are used optimally.					
(c) Confidential information is not disclosed to unauthorised people.					
(d) Risks to the information technology environments are minimised at all times.					
Range statement					
• Methods of requesting items: specification of unique reference codes, specification of details					
• Methods of locating details: automatic searching, manual searching (browsing)					
• Computer systems: databases, spreadsheets					
• Examples of databases: stock databases, customer databases, sales ledgers, purchase/bought ledgers, employee database and cash logs					
• Examples of recorded details of requested items: cost codes for a cost heading, type of payment of an order, progress and status of an order, credit limit/status/worthiness of a customer, employee details and grant codes for courses					

Assessment plan for Unit 20: Data processing

Element 3: Generate and print standard reports on a computer system

	Prior learning and experience	*Timing*	*Assessment methods*		*Portfolio Ref.*
Performance criteria			*APL*	*Other*	
(a) Required range and report correctly specified.					
(b) Printed information is correct and complete.					
(c) Hard copy is clean, clearly printed and aligned correctly.					
(d) Efforts are made to minimise the wastage of paper.					
(e) Printer area is kept clean and tidy.					
(f) Work is produced to agreed deadline.					
(g) Documents are correctly collated and distributed as directed.					
(h) Risks to the information technology environment are minimised at all times.					
Range statement					
• Generation: specification of the start and finish of the range and selection of the required report					
• Standard report: bar charts, pie charts, histograms, standard database reports (some of which require special stationery)					
• Computer systems: databases, spreadsheets					
• Examples of standard database reports: invoices, payments, pay runs, statements of accounts, infringement reports and flexitime reports					

Deciding on assessment methods

Based upon your comments in the *Prior learning and experience* column, you should identify the method of assessment which is *most likely* to apply.

If you feel there is a sufficiently good match to offer your prior learning or experience as evidence of competence, you should tick the *APL* column. If you have no previous experience or your experience is not sufficiently relevant, you should put a cross in the *APL* column. You should consider each of the *performance criteria* individually, asking yourself the following questions. Where you feel that your answers to the all the questions relating to performance criteria are satisfactory, you should put a tick in the APL column.

- How closely does my experience match the performance criteria? For example, do I have experience across the whole range specified?
- Did I carry out this activity frequently enough to be considered competent?
- How much assistance, if any, did I require to complete this task?
- Where my experience was in the past, could I still carry out the same task to the same level of competence today?
- Where my experience was in the past, is this area of work subject to frequent changes? Have I kept up to date with those changes?

Other methods of assessment

For each of the performance criteria against which there is a cross, you must now decide the best method of collecting evidence. If there are only a few gaps, maybe this is an area in which you could arrange for further experience as part of your current work or work placement.

If there are only one or two gaps, your AAC may accept a simulation. This Study Pack contains examples of simulations.

Complete the *Other methods* column with brief details of the most likely method.

(**Note:** Remember that what you have drawn up is simply a plan and you may alter this at any time during the assessment process, for example, if you gain further work experience against any of the performance criteria or as a result of discussions with your AAC.)

Assessment and study

Your next step is to agree your assessment plan with your AAC and to decide when assessment will take place as part of your broader study programme.

You should now start work on your *accounting portfolio*.

You may wish to use the planning document as the basis for your accounting portfolio by completing the final column *Portfolio reference*.

PREPARING AN ACCOUNTING PORTFOLIO

Objective

As we saw earlier, your accounting portfolio will be a collection of evidence which you have gathered together to demonstrate to the assessor that you are competent in your chosen elements.

As we saw above, your *accounting portfolio* will consist of:

- evidence of prior learning and experience
- current workplace evidence
- simulations

Using the assessment plan which you drew up above, we can now think about what might be included in the accounting portfolio. Once you have identified what might be included, the best approach is to gather evidence gradually over a period of time. Many people find it easiest to keep a file at work into which they put a copy of each piece of evidence as it arises. You will also need to allocate some time to actually compiling the portfolio.

The best approach is to complete one unit at a time. You should submit for assessment all the evidence relating to a single unit or group of units *at the same time*.

Essentially, your portfolio will be a collection of documents, selected by you which you feel are sufficient to demonstrate your competence in the performance criteria.

Most of these documents will probably be photocopies of actual pieces of work completed as part of your work or as part of a work placement. You may also wish to include evidence of other qualifications, including copies of certificates and syllabuses, accompanied by a short explanation of their relevance to the standards.

You may also find that you need to complete simulations.

Each piece of evidence must be accompanied by a completed *commentary sheet* which you will find in your *Student Record Book*. Do not forget that the accounting portfolio also provides evidence of your communications skills which are seen as an important part of all assessments at all stages.

UNIT 20

Contents

Let us now look at specific examples of evidence which you could include in a portfolio. We shall look in particular at Unit 20 *Data processing*.

The following items might be found in a candidate's portfolio. Note that it might not be necessary to include all of these types of evidence, neither is this an all-inclusive list of possible evidence.

- Photocopies of the candidate's diary of accounting work undertaken, highlighting tasks relating to data processing

- A description of an unusual transaction (unidentified cash receipt) and the steps taken by the candidate to identify the debtor account

- Extracts from the organisation's procedures manual concerning the security arrangements over the information technology environment, plus a description prepared by the candidate describing their involvement in those procedures and their implementation

- Copies of a database prepared and input by the candidate, accompanied by a short description of the procedures carried out and details of how inputting errors were corrected

- Copy of sales invoices and accompanying stock ledger adjustment on processing a sales transaction and a description of how the transactions are reflected in the nominal ledger

- A copy of a report prepared by a working party on the feasibility of using a payroll package accompanied by a description of the candidate's involvement

- A signed statement prepared by the candidate and signed by a supervisor, detailing the work carried out in their employment

- A copy of a certificate from another accounting qualification (completed six months earlier) and a copy of the syllabus which includes data processing, accompanied by a short description prepared by the candidate explaining the relevance to the standards

- A simulation

Notice how the candidate has made the relevance of each of the items to their experience clear, for example by including a description of their involvement or of the actual procedures carried out.

Note: Employer statements must give detailed descriptions of work carried out and its relevance to the standards. They are unlikely to be accepted in isolation. It is not acceptable for employers to submit a simple statement declaring an individual's competence in the place of an accounting portfolio. In addition, it is not acceptable for anyone other than a representative from your AAC to sign off your *Student Record Book*.

A note about confidentiality

You may have concerns about submitting copies of confidential documents as part of your accounting portfolio. In all cases, you are advised to seek permission from your employer and to remove as appropriate (with liquid paper) any sensitive information.

If there are further problems of confidentiality, you should consider submitting detailed descriptions of actual work undertaken, signed by your employer and supported by simulations.

If in doubt, you should always discuss the best method of assessment for you with your AAC.

Format and presentation

You are advised to use a lever arch file as the volume of documentation may be considerable.

Presentation is an important part of your accounting portfolio. All documents should be neat and tidy, with careful indexing and cross-referencing. A checklist is given below which you may find useful to ensure that your accounting portfolio contains the basic information required for assessment.

The assessment process

Your accounting portfolio will be assessed, one unit at a time, against the standards. In most cases, the assessment process will involve a short interview.

There are two possible outcomes of the process: you will be assessed as either *competent* or *not yet competent*. In the case of the latter, you will receive feedback as to where improvements need to be made within your accounting portfolio and invited to re-submit it at a later date.

(**Note:** Grades are not awarded for accounting portfolios.)

Accounting portfolio completion checklist

Overall format and contents

Are your name, address, AAT registration number, AAC number and the identity of the units attempted clearly shown on the file?

Have all documents been numbered?

Have you included a list of all the documents within the portfolio?

Have you supplied a list of all the performance criteria for this unit, cross-referenced to the relevant evidence?

Have all the performance criteria been covered by the evidence included within the portfolio?

Does each piece of work have a completed commentary sheet attached?

Does the portfolio contain a signed statement (or statements) from your supervisor/manager that your contribution to each piece of work has been accurately recorded and that permission has been given to include certain documents?

Individual pieces of work

Does each piece of work have a clear title and show the date of its preparation (eg. sales ledger reconciliation as at 31 July 19X5 of Alpha Co Ltd prepared on 1 August 19X5)?

Are the commentaries neatly and clearly presented?

Is it clear, in every case, exactly what your contribution was to the piece of work?

Is it clear how each piece of work demonstrates your competence in the particular performance criteria?

If you answer *No* to any of these questions, then you should not submit your portfolio without supplying this additional detail.

PREPARING FOR SIMULATION

What will the simulation cover?

Most simulations will cover either complete units or selected elements. Where you only require a simulation to cover certain performance criteria, you may find that your AAC still requires you to sit a simulation covering a complete element or unit as it may not be possible to assess those performance criteria out of context.

A typical simulation covering all the Unit 20 elements would require you to carry out accounting tasks as well as prepare a short business communication, such as replying to a letter or preparing a memorandum.

How much preparation is required?

You must be confident that you are competent in all the relevant performance criteria before attempting the simulation. A list of the likely tasks to be included in a simulation covering all the elements of Unit 20 *Data processing* is shown below. You should use this as a checklist to ensure that you have covered all areas. You should also attempt (or revise) the *practice simulation* within this Study Pack.

Remember that there is no pass mark for simulations: you are either assessed as *competent* or *not yet competent*. This means that you should aim to complete every task with complete accuracy. In fact, a few minor errors may be allowed, but this can only be decided by the assessor.

How long will it last?

There is no set time period for a simulation, although most take between three and four hours to complete. There is a time limit; the aim, however, is not to put you under unrealistic time-pressure, but to ensure that you can complete tasks in a reasonable period of time.

What is the assessor looking for?

While preparing for simulation, it is worth considering what the assessor is looking for. Remember that the assessor will assess you as either *competent* or *not yet competent*. To give you an indication of the general level required, ask yourself whether your supervisor/manager would be satisfied with a particular piece of work if you submitted it for review. Remember that the simulation is meant to simulate real work tasks, so the same standards must apply.

If we consider a typical simulation for Unit 20 *Data processing*, the assessor will be looking for evidence of good presentation skills, completeness, good communication skills, accuracy and technical knowledge.

Good presentation skills

All work should be neat and well presented, as if it were real work. You should use black ink or biro. Pencil is not acceptable, neither is correcting fluid (eg. Tipp-Ex). Cross out any errors neatly and clearly. Always use a ruler for underlining.

Completeness

All tasks should be complete (for example, columns totalled). Unlike in other forms of test, you cannot decide to leave out part of an exercise and still hope to be successful.

Good communication skills

Communication skills are fundamentally important in all the assessments for all stages. You are expected to show a good standard of English, including correct spelling and correct use of accounting terms.

Accuracy

All calculations must be completed accurately (for example, the calculation of the tax on a salary). All documents completed (for example, cheques) must be accurate. All accounting entries must be correct.

All discrepancies and exceptions must be identified and dealt with correctly. At Foundation stage, this normally means referring them to someone at supervisor level.

Technical knowledge

Any explanations given – for example, how VAT works – must be accurate.

PREPARING FOR DEVOLVED ASSESSMENT

Data-processing

You must be familiar with the following general processes applicable to data-processing:

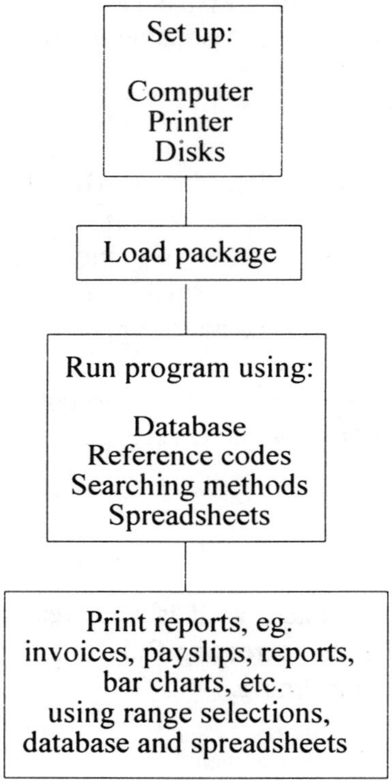

All the time risks to the IT environment must be minimised so *save* your work regularly and back up your disks.

You must ensure that you are competent at running a computer accounting system and can achieve *all* the performance criteria.

CENTRAL ASSESSMENT

There is only one central assessment at Foundation stage (*Cash and credit*) which covers both Unit 1 *recording and accounting for cash transactions* and Unit 2 *Recording and accounting for credit transactions*.

There is no central assessment for Unit 20.

THE ROLE OF STUDY

Studying for different reasons

Finally, we need to consider the role of study within the scheme. Whatever your previous experience, you will inevitably need to devote a considerable amount of time to studying, even if it is only to familiarise yourself with the coverage of the devolved assessment. This Study Pack contains study and practice material covering all the performance criteria and knowledge and understanding required for this unit.

The objective of this Study Pack is to provide you with:

- guidance on completing the assessments for this unit
- examples of best practice as a reference when preparing your *accounting portfolio*
- study materials and practice materials for areas in which you have no prior experience in which you are required to sit a simulation

USING THIS STUDY PACK

Whatever your previous experience, you are therefore encouraged to work through the Study Pack, paying attention to the areas which are most relevant to you. Here is a short explanation of the aim of each aspect of this Study Pack and the areas in which they are relevant.

- *Sessions 1–7:* Contain study material and examples on a particular topic to help you learn the required techniques. The relevant performance criteria are identified at the start of each session. In addition, the knowledge and understanding required for that topic are included within that session.
- *Assignments:* Practice simulation material covering selected performance criteria. The assignments are graded in difficulty and cover selected elements only to help you build up the required skills gradually.
- *Simulations:* Full simulations covering all the Unit 20 elements. The simulation is designed to be as difficult as, if not more difficult than, the real simulation which you will have to sit. This means that, if you are competent in this simulation, you are well prepared for the real thing!

FURTHER STUDY MATERIAL

The Financial Training Company also publishes a *Central Assessment Pack* designed to give you additional practice towards the *cash and credit* central assessment. As well as containing new exercises of the sort featured in the real central assessments, it also contains brief revision notes of all major topics.

Central Assessment Packs are available from your usual supplier of Financial Training Company study materials.

PUBLISHER'S NOTE

Financial Training study materials are distributed in the UK and overseas by Stanley Thornes (Publishers) Limited. They are another company within the Wolters Kluwer group. They can be contacted at: Stanley Thornes, Ellenborough House, Wellington Street, Cheltenham GL50 1YD. Telephone: (01242) 228888. Fax: (01242) 221914.

Introduction to computer skills

WHAT ARE YOU TRYING TO ACHIEVE?

This course is about using computers to process accounting information. You will use your chosen software packages to learn more about this area. Remember that this unit is particularly relevant to work as most businesses use computers as part of their accounting systems

Before starting this course it is important to identify why you are going to process accounting information by electronic means.

What do *you* think the advantages of processing information by computer are?

You may be able to:

- process data more quickly than by manual methods;
- process data more accurately;
- analyse information more efficiently and effectively;
- generate reports more efficiently and effectively.

It is important to remember that computers cannot replace all parts of a manual accounting system. It is also important to remember that the quality of the *analysis* and *report-generation* performed by the computer will depend very much upon the *quality* of the information input by the operator.

As you are working through this course you should be asking yourself the following questions.

- Which manual ledgers are replaced by the software packages I am using?

- Which operations are performed automatically?

- Which reports or analyses are generated or performed automatically, reducing the risk of error (eg. in preparing a report manually there is a risk of transposition or other errors)?

- At which points is there a risk of *error* and what can be done to *control* this risk?

DIFFERENT TYPES OF HARDWARE

The hardware you are using will vary depending upon the size and type of organisation which you are working for.

PERSONAL COMPUTER: Machines which are small enough to sit on a desk top. Some are even small enough to be portable.

LOCAL AREA NETWORK: A system linking individual computers within one building allowing users to share facilities (eg. printers), to have access to same the programs and files, or to communicate with each other.

MAINFRAME: A complex computer with a large memory. Such a system can have hundreds of individual users. This type of system is used by large companies, banks, building societies and local government.

Whichever type of hardware you are using, they all have one thing in common: the processes carried out by the computer are dependent upon the *software* in use.

Let us assume that you are using a PC. Your PC will have at least one *disk drive* and perhaps a hard disk as well.

Let us consider a *twin-floppy* PC. This type of machine has two disk drives (slots at the front of the PC) into which *floppy disks* are inserted. The disk drives can *read* the disks.

These floppy disks contain the software (*or programs*) necessary to carry out the processing. The programs are essentially a set of instructions to the computer. Without those instructions the computer cannot operate.

The user is prompted by the machine to insert the required disks into the disk drives at certain points of the operation. With this type of PC no information is stored within the machine for longer than the time that it takes to carry out the processes prompted by the program which is used. In other words the machine itself has no long-term built-in *memory*.

Let us compare this type of PC to one with a *hard disk*. A machine with a hard disk has two (or more drives): a floppy-disk drive (used to *load programs* onto the hard disk or to export programs or files from the hard disk) and a hard disk drive (used to store loaded programs).

The advantages of using a machine with a hard disk are that more complex processes can be carried out and that programs do not have to be loaded every time the machine is used. The hard disk has a *memory* (ie. when the machine is switched off, the hard disk still retains the programs and information stored on it).

DIFFERENT TYPES OF SOFTWARE

Let us assume you are using a PC with a *hard disk*. The PC needs two types of software to run: the *operating system* and the *application programs*.

OPERATING SYSTEM: A series of programs which form a link between the hardware and the application programs and which provide the user with certain basic functions.

The operating system makes it easier for the user to use the system. For example, before an application program can be run, it must be loaded into the computer's *main memory*. This is a complex task, but the user is generally unaware of this as it is carried out by the operating system.

Other functions include allowing the user to *back-up* files or to *copy* files.

APPLICATION PROGRAMS: These are the specific programs which are chosen by the individual user to carry out certain tasks.

The application programs which you are most likely to come across are:

- databases;
- spreadsheets;
- word-processing packages; and
- accounting packages.

DATABASE: This is a method of sorting information in such a way that the user can access and rearrange it to produce meaningful data.

A database can contain the information which could be stored in a large filing cabinet.

The files contain individual records. Think of these as individual card files listing all the data related to one item (eg. a customer's details). If you were using a card-file system you would have to choose one order to store the cards (eg. *alphabetical order*), although you could use *cross-referencing cards* for certain entries.

This would mean that you could only look up information easily if you knew the name of the customer. It would be possible, but time-consuming and inefficient, to extract any other information (eg. all customers within a certain town).

A database makes it easier to perform this sort of task as it is able to do all the sorting and searching much more quickly and efficiently.

Information is added through *forms* displayed on the screen. Some databases are set up in advance and therefore are not expected to be modified (see *accounting packages* below), others are blank shells to be customised by the individual user.

SPREADSHEET: A framework which is used to handle numbers with ease.

A spreadsheet consists of a grid or table of *cells* each one of which can have a *value* or an *instruction* put into it. The instruction can be *add*, *subtract*, *multiply* or *divide*, a *combination* of these instructions or to perform a function (eg. calculate the square root).

WORD-PROCESSING PACKAGE: A package which allows the user to type and edit documents.

These packages are more flexible than using a typewriter because:

- *errors* can be corrected on the screen before the document is printed out;
- the package can offer the user help with the *format* of documents;
- documents can be checked for *spelling errors*; and
- personalised versions of documents (eg. letters) can be produced from the same basic document without re-typing the entire document. This is particularly efficient if the package is used with a database which can provide names and addresses to avoid re-typing them.

ACCOUNTING PACKAGE: A program which is based on a database. The database is set up in advance and is unlikely to be modified by the user.

These are the packages which you will use when completing the performance criteria for this unit. Most accounting packages are *menu-driven*. This means that they guide you through the various parts of the program by presenting you with options from which you must choose where you want to go.

The best way to learn how to use these programs is to practise. Always read the manual before starting and refer to it if you have any problems.

This Study Pack is not designed to tell you which buttons to push. It is designed to help you 'explore' your chosen programs through a series of case studies and assignments.

GETTING STARTED

Whatever type of computer system you are using you will need certain basic skills to be able to use it to its full potential. You will need to be able to:

- input information using the *keyboard*;
- interpret information shown on the *screen*; and
- print out reports using a *printer*.

Let us look first at the keyboard.

The keyboard to your computer is based on a typewriter keyboard. It has the same basic layout of keys as a typewriter. The main difference is that it has extra keys. The main additional keys may include:

Backspace key	Used to erase the character to the left of the cursor
Function keys	Extra keys which have different uses depending upon the software you are using
Return key	Like the return on a typewriter, it is some times used to move to the next line. It is also used to mark the end of an entry.
Direction/calculator keys	These keys have two functions depending upon whether or not the *number lock* is used. With number lock they become a calculator. *Without* number lock they move the cursor around the screen. (Note how you can go down one page or up one page by pressing one key.)
Direction keys	Some keyboards have an additional set of direction keys
Escape key	Used in certain programs to move between different levels of the program

SOME IMPORTANT POINTS

Let us look at certain areas which you should be aware of *before* you start to use your chosen packages. These are:

- care of disks;
- using write-protect;
- making back-up copies;
- security and confidentiality;
- maintenance; and
- health and safety.

Care of disks

You will be using floppy disks which are of the size used by your particular machine. These will be either 3½" or 5¼" disks.

The 5¼" disks have a flexible casing and are quite delicate. You must not bend these disks as you will damage them and you will be unable to use them. Do not touch the disk inside its protective plastic shell. You should also keep these disks in their paper sleeves.

The 3½" disks have a rigid plastic cover.

Whichever disks you are using, you must store them in a clean, dry place, such as a disk box (a specially designed plastic tray). If you leave them lying on your desk they may have something put on top of them or have coffee spilt on them.

Keep the disks away from electrical equipment as this may scramble the information on the disk.

If you are using floppy disks do not write on labels which are already stuck to the disks as the pressure from the pen may damage the disk.

Using write-protect

Disks are like cassette tapes or video tapes: they can be bought for what is already on them, or you can use them to record something of your choice. Also like tapes you may want to avoid losing something by recording over it. Cassette tapes and video tapes allow you to stop this from happening and so do disks. This is vital if you want to protect programs which you have bought or data which you cannot recreate.

Floppy disks have a notch which you must cover up with a small sticky label. The machine will detect the label and stop you from overwriting the files on the disk.

Rigid disks have a small tab in one corner which slides across. The machine will check the tab before over-writing the contents of the disk.

Making back-up copies

If you are using a *twin-floppy* you will have to store all your data on disk and re-input it next time you want to run your program again. If you damage these disks you will have lost all your work; therefore you should make extra back-up copies on different disks each time you leave the system.

Even if you are using a machine with a hard disk, the hard disk may sometimes develop a fault. You should make regular back-up copies even if you are using a hard disk.

Security and confidentiality

The system which you are using (particularly if you are one of many users on a *network* or *mainframe*) may contain confidential information. Think of it as a filing cabinet full of documents. If it were a filing cabinet you would want to lock it. The computer equivalents of locking the cabinet include:

- using passwords to restrict access;
- restricting user access to certain parts of the system only;

- storing confidential information in a particular directory (a directory is like a drawer in the filing cabinet);
- storing disks containing confidential information in a separate disk tray.

Maintenance

It is important to keep your computer clean if it is to work properly. There are special products available to clean the machine. *Never* use ordinary household cleaning products.

The screen should be wiped with a special anti-static *screen-wipe*. The keyboard should be kept free from dust with a *keyboard brush*. Any marks on the computer casing should be removed with a special *cleaner*.

Health and safety

Health and safety is covered more generally elsewhere but it is worth repeating the main points relating to the use of computers and VDUs (*Visual Display Units*).

Remember that like any other piece of electrical equipment you should observe basic safety (eg. do not leave trailing flexes or overload plugs). Remember that repairs on electrical equipment should only be carried out by a qualified electrical technician.

Certain aspects of data processing present a particular risk to the health of individuals. If you spend a large part of your working day working at a VDU you risk various problems including eye strain, back problems and RSI (*Repetitive Strain Injury*). RSI appears to arise from making the same movements over and over again, and affects hands and arms.

If you ever suffer any pain or discomfort while working at a VDU then you must take a break. It would also help if you could move on to a task not involving the VDU.

If you work at a VDU there are certain things you can do to reduce the risk of problems.

- Use a five-leg swivel chair (preferably with an adjustable back rest) set at the correct height.
- Sit with the keyboard and monitor *directly* in front of you. (Do not sit in a position which means you have to turn your head to see the screen.)
- Adjust the monitor so that it is on the same level as your eyes.
- Avoid a position which means there is light reflected directly from windows.
- Sit with your feet slightly raised on a support or book.
- Use the keyboard in its *flat* position. Your forearms should be level with the work surface and your wrists should rest on the work surface.
- Make sure you have enough space on your work station for books and papers you are working on. Tidy away any other items which you are not actually using.
- Take regular breaks and avoid looking at the screen continuously for long periods of time.

DATA PROTECTION ACT 1984

The increasing use of computers in all aspects of business has meant that increasingly large amounts of information about individuals are now kept by various organisations.

There is a risk that some of this information is *inaccurate* which could cause serious problems for the individual concerned (eg. they may be refused a loan if they have the wrong credit rating). To help reduce this risk, the Data Protection Act was introduced.

The *Data Protection Registrar* keeps a register of companies who hold information on computer. Each company which falls into this category must register of its own accord.

A copy of the Data Protection Register is held in all major libraries.

Any unregistered data-user who holds personal data, which is not exempt, commits a criminal offence, the maximum penalty for which is an unlimited fine.

Principles of data protection

Registered data-users must comply with the following principles which broadly state that personal data shall be:

- obtained and processed, fairly and lawfully
- held only for the lawful purposes described in the register entry
- used only for those purposes and only be disclosed to those people described in the register entry
- adequate, relevant and not excessive in relation to the purposes for which it is held
- accurate and, where necessary, kept up to date
- held no longer than is necessary for that purpose or purposes
- surrounded by proper security

An individual shall be entitled:

- at reasonable intervals and without undue delay or expense:
  - to be informed by any data-user whether he holds personal data of which that individual is the subject
  - to access any such data held by the data user
- where appropriate, to have such data corrected or erased

Exemptions to the Act

The Act does not apply to all personal data and the following are exempt:

- Personal data held by an individual in connection with personal, family or recreational purposes

This exemption will not apply to an individual who keeps records on behalf of a club, church or voluntary organisation. Then the organisation, rather than the individual, will be the data-user. The individual will not need to register but the organisation may need to do so.

- Information that the law requires to make public

  For example, the Companies Act 1985 requires every registered company to make its registration of members available to public inspection.

- Payrolls, pensions and accounts purposes

  This exemption does not apply if the data is used for wider purposes, such as for personnel records or for marketing purposes.

- National security

  Exemption at the discretion of the government minister

- Mailing lists are exempt as long as the personal data only consists of names, addresses and other details needed for distribution, such as phone number, fax number, etc. The data subject must be asked if they object to the data being held for this purpose.

- Unincorporated members' clubs (eg. sports clubs which are not registered companies)

  All the data subjects must be members of the club and must agree to the data being held for this purpose. The personal data about members may only be disclosed in very limited circumstances.

Many of the exemptions are conditional. If the condition is not observed, the exemption does not apply.

The effect of exemptions on those upon whom data is held:

- The personal data is not registered.
- The individual has no right of access to the personal data; however, if access to the data is requested, the user must always reply.
- The registrar has no power under the Act; however, the courts may inspect the data if an individual applies to them suspecting that the data is not exempt.

Individual rights

- **Subject access right** entitles individuals to a copy of the information which forms the personal data held about them by the data-user. Requests for subject access should be made in writing and sent to the data-user at the address given in the register entry. The data-user may charge a fee for dealing with a subject access request.

- **Right to take action for compensation** if the individual is damaged by inaccurate personal data or by loss or unauthorised destruction or disclosure of personal data. An application for compensation must be made by the individual to the County Court or High Court. The Registrar cannot award compensation. The term *damage* includes financial loss and physical injury but does not include distress suffered by the individual.

- **Right to take action** to have inaccurate personal data corrected or erased. The data subject may apply to the County Court or High Court for an order that the data-user should correct or erase the data. A Registrar can also order the correction or erasure but the court's powers are wider than the Registrar's. *Inaccurate* means incorrect or misleading about any matter of fact, not an opinion.

- **Right to complain** to the Registrar that any of the data protection principles or any other provision of the Act has been broken. Many individuals prefer to have their complaints investigated by the Registrar rather than incur the expense and trouble of court proceedings.

WHERE DO YOU START?

You may need to load the software packages if they are not already loaded on to your system.

To do this, follow the *manuals* for both your computer system and your chosen software.

Load your ledger package.

Your package *may* ask you to give details of the company or business you wish to set up. (If you do not appear to need it, ignore these details.) Remember that you should only delete this data once you have finished with a particular section of the Study Pack. The Study Pack will tell you when to set up the next entity.

Here are the details of the company we are going to look at in this first case study. Input these details carefully. The easiest way to correct errors is to use the *backspace* key.

Company name	Greensleeves Ltd
Address	123 Greenwood Road Withington Manchester M20 4TF
Telephone	0161 460 7488
Fax	0161 460 3442
VAT reg. no.	456 3344 12
Debtors accounts needed	20
Creditors accounts needed	20
Product accounts needed	20

If your program asks you to choose from these options:

1 debtors' (or sales) ledger and creditors'(or purchase) ledger *only*; or
2 debtors' and creditors' ledger plus nominal ledger

choose *option* 2.

The Sage Educational package will not allow you to input any company name as, by default, it prints *Sage Educational* for the company name. This cannot be changed so continue as usual to complete each exercise; your mark will not be affected by this.

This case study looks at a *limited company*.

You will now be faced with a menu of options. But where do you start as none of the data files contain any information?

Let us start by visualising how the program works. Let us think of it in terms of a manual system.

In a manual system, you would find the following books of prime entry:

- cash book
- petty cash book
- sales day book
- sales returns day book
- purchase day book
- purchase returns day book
- journal

You would also find the following ledgers:

- debtors' ledger
- creditors' ledger
- nominal ledger

In a manual system, you would find the following information:

- standing data (eg. customer names and addresses, nominal ledger codes)
- opening balances brought forward
- transactions in the current period

Within a computerised system you will find the same basic components, although they may be slightly different depending upon the program you use. For example, some packages do not have a detailed cash book.

First let us revise accounting systems. Remember that the double-entry system is contained *only* within the *nominal ledger*.

Each transaction recorded in the *nominal ledger* must be recorded twice. This is the *dual effect*. For every debit there is an equal credit and for every credit a debit.

The nominal ledger contains *ledger accounts* in which the transactions are recorded. This makes it easier to summarise and analyse the transactions at month or year-end.

The *debtors'* and *creditors'* ledgers are memorandum accounts. This means that they are not part of the double entry. They contain the same information about debtors and creditors as you find in the nominal ledger, but the information is *analysed* in a different way.

The *books of prime entry* are diaries of the transactions. They are not part of the double-entry system, but they contain information which is repeated within the nominal ledger.

DEALING WITH CREDIT SALES

Let us look first at *credit sales*.

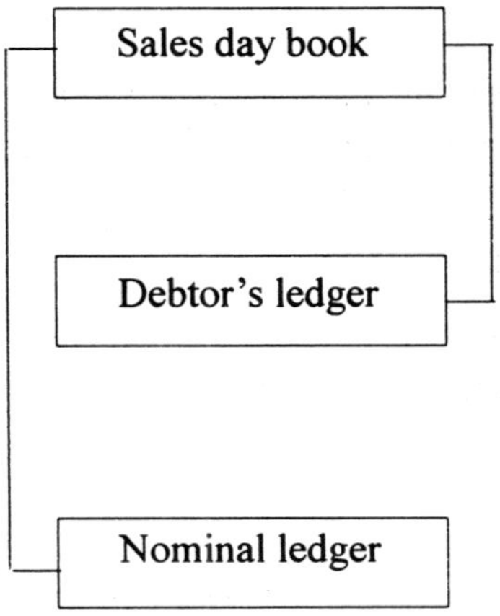

Sales are entered into sales day book

Transactions are automatically posted to the debtors' ledger

Transactions are automatically posted to the nominal ledger

Note how the debtors' ledger and nominal ledger are updated independently from the same source. This is how your ledger program works in outline. You will input the details of the credit sales (invoices) into the sales input screen and the program will update the ledgers automatically.

Some programs also have the ability to generate the original invoices. We will also look at that later.

DEALING WITH CREDIT PURCHASES

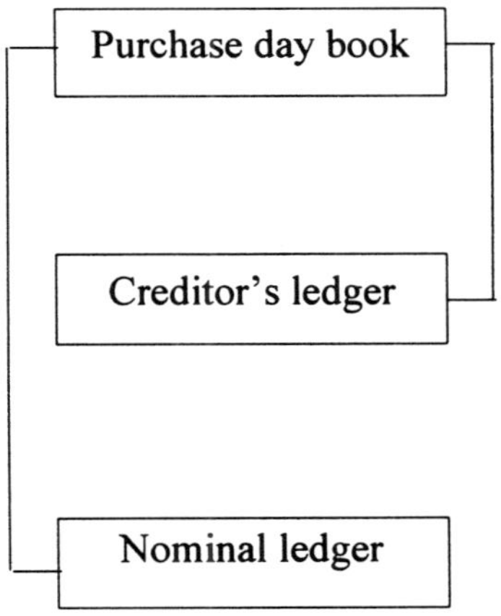

Purchases are entered into purchases day book

Transactions are automatically posted to the creditors' ledger

Transactions are automatically posted to the nominal ledger

The system for recording credit purchases is identical to the system for recording credit sales.

RECORDING CASH RECEIPTS

Most packages do not have a separate cash book. How they work is that receipts from debtors are input through a special screen which records the receipts in the debtors' ledger and the nominal ledger in much the same way as credit sales.

Other types of receipts (which are not from debtors) must be input directly into the nominal ledger (normally via the *journal* or a special cash posting screen).

This also applies to petty cash transactions.

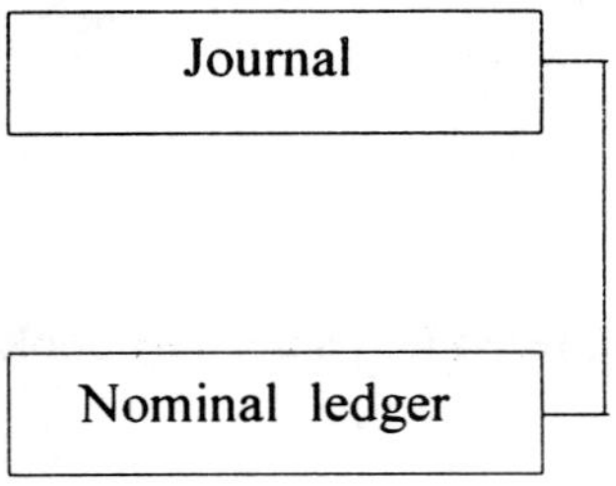

Receipts are entered into the journal or special screen

Transactions are automatically posted to the nominal ledger

RECORDING CASH PAYMENTS

Cash payments (whether from a bank account or from petty cash) must be divided into two types: payments to creditors and other payments.

The two types of payment are then input into two different parts of the program (as above with receipts). Payments to creditors are input through a special screen in the creditors' ledger option. Other payments are input by journal or by a special screen in the nominal ledger option.

> ***Question***
>
> *Which receipts and payments might a business have other than receipts from debtors and payments to creditors?*

Recording and accounting for cash transactions

COLLECTING STANDING DATA

This first case study is about a small business which sells environmentally friendly adult and children's clothing.

The company is registered for VAT but has not yet started trading. The business intends to make both cash and credit sales and purchases.

The business has five prospective customers and five prospective suppliers. The credit limit for each account is £1,000.00 and the VAT code for all of them is GB.

Customers

Fred Brown Associates
234 Barlow Moor Road
West Didsbury
Manchester
M19 5DG

Telephone:	0161 456 8833	Contact:	Fred Brown
VAT No:	888 999 0101 22		

Everett Enterprises
122 Wilbraham Road
Chorlton
Manchester
M21 9JK

Telephone:	0161 860 3345	Contact:	Sid Francis
VAT No:	070 545 2233 01		

Thornwood Manufacturing Ltd
89 Glendale Street
Ancoats
Manchester
M1 3GH

Telephone:	0161 236 1903	Contact:	Sarah Marshall
VAT No:	200 200 6666 05		

Taylor and Atkins
34 Lightbowne Road
Moston
Manchester
M15 1TF

Telephone:	0161 556 4785	Contact:	Steve Hardy
VAT No:	123 456 7777 88		

White Brothers
239 Darnell Way
Oldham
OL1 4NM

Telephone:	0161 940 3782	Contact:	Heather Thomas
VAT No:	999 000 1234 55		

Suppliers

Trevor Manufacturing Ltd
345 Taylforth Road
Sale
Manchester
M24 2KN

Telephone:	0161 345 2234	Contact:	Harold Goodman
VAT No:	333 444 5555 66		

Olympic Design Studio
34 Weaver Street Withington
Manchester
M20 2JL

Telephone:	0161 404 4654	Contact:	Betty Davies
VAT No:	777 888 9999 01		

Joseph Parker & Sons
7 Hillside Drive
Chorlton
Manchester
M21 4DF

Telephone:	0161 403 5712	Contact:	Laura Jackson
VAT No:	112 333 4545 66		

Hill and Saint
566 Burton Road
Withington
Manchester
M20 8JN

Telephone:	0161 723 3887	Contact:	Kevin Birch
VAT No:	777 888 9090 11		

Fryer Supplies Ltd
899 Regency Way
Bolton
BL1 4RT

Telephone: 01204 5734 Contact: David Warren
VAT No: 222 345 6789 22

Nominal codes

The codes which will be needed are as follows

4000	Sales type A
5009	Discounts taken
5000	Materials purchases
4009	Discounts allowed
6900	Miscellaneous expenses
1100	Debtors control account
2200	Tax control account (VAT)
1200	Bank current account (cash at bank)
1230	Petty cash
2100	Creditors control account
3000	Ordinary shares
1001	Stock

INPUTTING STANDING DATA

Which data will you need to input before you can get started?

This will be:

- customer names, addresses and account numbers; and
- supplier names, addresses and account numbers;
- nominal ledger codes.

Identify which part of your program you need to use to input this standing data.

Customers' details

Suppliers' details

Complete each screen carefully. Number the accounts from 00001 to 00005 and use the Help function when you need more explanations. Once you have input all the details, print out a list of customers and a list of suppliers. If you have more than one reports option, try printing out all of the reports. (This may include sorting the entries in different orders.)

Enter the print commands here.

Customers

Suppliers

The exercises which follow use *number order* to identify customers and suppliers.

Nominal codes

You may find that your program already has nominal codes set up. You may use these if you prefer.

Print out the nominal ledger codes. Enter the commands here.

Recording the first transaction

The first entry you need to post is to record the shares bought by the owner. He has bought £10,000 of share capital. He has introduced £7,500 in cash and stock of £2,500.

Question 1

What is the double-entry for this transaction?

	Code	£
Dr		
Cr		

How will you input this into your program?

A note on nominal ledger codes

When assigning nominal codes you will probably also have to allocate them to particular sections of the financial statements. It is very important that you get this classification right. (See Appendix 2.)

POSTING SALES INVOICES

Here are the sales invoices for the first month of trading. Do not worry about dates for this exercise.

No.	*Customer*	*Net* £	*VAT* £	*Gross* £
1	Everett Enterprises	245.00	42.88	287.88
2	Taylor and Atkins	45.37	7.94	53.31
3	Thornwood Manufacturing	137.99	24.15	162.14
4	White Brothers	49.26	8.62	57.88
5	Taylor and Atkins	87.20	15.26	102.46

You are required to post these into the correct part of your program. Which option do you need in your program?

Make sure you complete each *field* (ie. section, box or space) correctly. Check the details carefully before you go on to the next screen.

You should allocate these invoices to the *standard rate* VAT code and the *sales* account in the nominal ledger.

Question 2

What is the double-entry for the total of these transactions?

Remember that although you have only input the sales invoice details into a screen, the program has completed the double entry for you.

The program has also updated the individual accounts in the debtors' ledger.

Question 3

Why has the total amount invoiced (including VAT) been debited to debtors?

Question 4

Why has the net amount (excluding VAT) been credited to sales?

Question 5

What do the following balances represent (ie, asset, liability, revenue, expense, capital) ?

- *Sales*
- *Debtors*
- *VAT (credit balance)*

POSTING PURCHASE INVOICES

Here is the first batch of purchase invoices.

No.	*Supplier*	*Net* £	*VAT* £	*Gross* £
1	Hill and Saint	123.76	21.66	145.42
2	Fryer Supplies Ltd	76.66	13.42	90.08
3	Joseph Parker & Sons	34.22	5.99	40.21
4	Hill and Saint	16.78	2.94	19.72
5	Trevor Manufacturing	68.34	11.96	80.30

Question 6

What is the double-entry for the total of these transactions?

Note that you must debit purchases (*never* stock).

Remember that although you have only input the purchase invoice details into a screen, the program has completed the double entry for you.

The program has also updated the individual accounts in the creditors' ledger.

Question 7

What is the disadvantage of inputting sale or purchase invoices into a program through a special screen rather than recording them in a sales day book?

How can this problem be solved?

DRAFT TRIAL BALANCE

You have now completed posting the first batches of transactions.

Question 8

Look back over the transactions you have posted and work out what the trial balance looks like at the end of the month.

Here is a pro forma to help you. Remember you must decide if each balance is a debit or a credit.

Greensleeves Ltd
Trial balance

		Dr	Cr
		£	£
1001	Stock		
1100	Debtors control		
1200	Bank		
1230	Petty cash		
2100	Creditors control		
2200	Tax control		
3000	Ordinary shares		
4000	Sales type A		
4009	Discounts allowed		
5000	Materials purchases		
5009	Discounts taken		
6900	Miscellaneous expenses		

Now print out the trial balance. It should be the same as the trial balance above.

Question 9

Print out the individual accounts in the debtors' ledger and creditors' ledger. Note how they add up to the same balance as the total on the debtors and creditors accounts in the nominal ledger.

Why must this be the case?

Record the printing commands here.

RECORDING CASH RECEIPTS

Let us move on in time. Let us assume the customers all pay the full amount. (Again do not worry about the timescale for the moment.)

Cash receipts from debtors are recorded in the cash book as follows. (This could be a computerised log, but you will need a proper list of receipts and payments either computerised or manual to satisfy legal requirements.)

	£
Thornwood Manufacturing	162.14
Everett Enterprises	287.88
White Brothers	57.88
Taylor and Atkins	155.77

Question 10

What will the double-entry be to post the totals into the nominal ledger?

Which screen will you use to post these receipts?

Your package will probably ask you to specify the bank account into which the cash has been paid.

Use your package's *allocation facility* to pay off each invoice. Note how the receipt from Taylor and Atkins pays off two invoices.

When you have posted the receipts do not forget to print the audit trail.

Display the accounts in the debtors' ledger on the screen. Note how they have all been updated automatically.

Question 11

Which control procedure over cash receipts (and payments) would you carry out at least monthly?

Question 12

Where would you get information from customers as to which invoices they are paying off?

RECORDING CASH PAYMENTS

The cash book shows the following payments.

	Invoice No.	£
Hill and Saint	1	145.42
Fryer Supplies Ltd	2	90.08
Joseph Parker & Sons	3	40.21
Trevor Manufacturing	5	80.30

Which screen will you use to input these transactions?

Allocate the payments against the invoices you are paying off.

SETTLEMENT DISCOUNTS OFFERED TO CUSTOMERS

To improve cash flow let us offer a 2% settlement discount to customers who pay within 7 days.

Here is the next batch of sales invoices.

No.	*Customer*	*Net* £	*VAT* £	*Gross* £
6	Everett Enterprises	236.44	40.54	276.98
7	Fred Brown Associates	38.56	6.61	45.17
8	Taylor and Atkins	112.70	19.32	132.02

The VAT charge is based on the lowest amount the customer could pay (ie. 98% of the net value).

Post these transactions using the screen identified earlier.

The cash book later shows the following receipts.

	Cash	*Discount* £
Everett Enterprises	272.26	4.72
Fred Brown Associates	44.40	0.77
Taylor and Atkins	129.77	2.25

Post these transactions using the screen identified earlier.

Question 13

What is the double-entry to record the above receipts?

Question 14

Note how the cash paid plus the discount clears each invoice in full.

What would happen if the customer paid the full amount and did not take the discount? Would the customer pay the extra VAT?

TAKING ADVANTAGE OF SETTLEMENT DISCOUNTS

Let us look at an invoice from a new supplier who is prepared to give a settlement discount if the company settles its account within 10 days. There is a 1.5% settlement discount.

Here is the invoice from the supplier.

No.	*Supplier*	*Net* £	*VAT* £	*Gross* £
6	Farmer Manufacturing Ltd 122 High Lane Gorton M8 2DJ	167.88	28.93	196.81

Phone: 0161 345 7766 Contact: Wendy Hillby
VAT No: 987 654 3210 12

You will have to set up a new supplier account first, before processing this invoice.

Question 15

How much will the company pay the supplier, if it takes advantage of the discount?

Post this payment using the screen identified earlier.

Question 16

What is the double-entry to record the above payment?

SENDING OUT REMITTANCE ADVICES

Remittance advices can be printed by certain programs. Does your chosen program have this facility? How does it work?

Pay off the following invoice then print out the remittance advice.

	£
Hill and Saint	19.72

Greensleeves Ltd
123 Greenwood Road
Withington
Manchester
M20 4TF

Tel: 0161 4607 488

Hill and Saint
566 Burton Road
Withington
Manchester
M20 8JN

REMITTANCE ADVICE

ACC REF	4	DATE	*	TRANS REF		PAGE	1

DATE		REF		OUTSTANDING	PAID THIS MONTH	REMAINING	THIS PAYMENT
*	Inv	4		19.71	19.71		19.71

		TOTAL DUE	
19.71	19.71		19.71
		Total paid	19.71
		Less discount	
		Cheque enclosed	19.71

CASH SALES AND PURCHASES

Let us look at what would happen if the company made cash sales.

The cash book would show entries as follows.

Narrative	*Net* £	*VAT* £	*Gross* £
Cash sales	354.25	61.99	416.24

Question 17

What is the double-entry to record cash sales?

Question 18

Why is VAT analysed and accounted for at this stage? (Compare this with cash received from debtors.)

Which screen will you use to post these sales?

Post these cash sales.

The principle is the same for payments through the bank account which are made to non-credit suppliers. Here are some payments for you to post.

Narrative	*Net* £	*VAT* £	*Gross* £
Materials purchases	98.56	17.25	115.81
Miscellaneous expenses	34.44		34.44

The 'expenses' payment is VAT exempt.

Question 19

What is the double-entry to record these payments?

PETTY CASH PAYMENTS

The main source for petty cash is the main bank account. It has been estimated that the business needs £150 a month petty cash to cover minor cash expenses.

The business maintains a petty cash book in which payments are recorded (including the analysis of VAT where applicable).

The payments are summarised as follows.

Narrative	*Net* £	*VAT* £	*Gross* £
Purchases	22.34	2.46	24.80
Expenses	11.38	1.76	13.14

Question 20

What is the double-entry for the transfer of £150 from the main account to petty cash?

Question 21

What would be the source of information for this transfer?

Question 22

What is the double-entry to post the payments?

AT MONTH-END

Let us assume that all of these transactions have taken place in the first month of trading. The final trial balance should look like this:

Greensleeves Ltd
Trial balance

		Dr £	*Cr* £
1001	Stock	2,500.00	
1200	Bank current account	8,156.07	
1230	Petty cash	112.06	
2100	Creditors control account		0.00
2200	Tax control account		120.95
3000	Ordinary shares		10,000.00
4000	Sales type A		1,306.77
4009	Discounts allowed	5.23	
5000	Material purchases	608.54	
6000	Miscellaneous expenses	45.82	
1100	Debtors control	-	
		11,427.72	11,427.72

The next stage is to reset the accounts for the next period (eg. clear out invoices which have been paid off in full in the debtors' and creditors' ledgers). You must only do this if you have already printed out copies of all the accounts in the debtors' and creditors' ledgers. You will need these to refer to in the case of a query.

Your program may also offer you the chance to re-set the accounts at year-end. This should only be done at the end of the financial year.

MAKING CORRECTIONS AND DEALING WITH OPENING BALANCES

Sometimes it is not a good idea to go back and change entries even if you know there is an error. This is particularly true when you discover the error in the next accounting period (whether it is the next month or the next year).

In this case it is better to post an adjustment to correct the error. You could do this by inputting the difference through the same screen as the original data (eg. an additional invoice for an item despatched but not invoiced) or by cancelling the original entry and inputting the correct entry (eg. recording a credit note to cancel an incorrect invoice, then re-issuing the corrected invoice).

If you are setting up opening balances in the debtors' and creditors' ledgers you must use the following double entry.

The following example uses the debtors' ledger, but the same would apply to the creditors' ledger.

Let us assume that the business has the following opening balances.

	Dr	*Cr*
	£	£
Assets (excluding debtors)	3,345.67	
Debtors	1,234.89	
Liabilities		2,635.28
Capital		1,945.28
	4,580.56	4,580.56

Stage one

When inputting the outstanding items (sales invoices and credit notes) the nominal code is *Suspense* or *Opening balances* (say account 9998).

	Dr	*Cr*
	£	£
Debtors	1,234.89	
Suspense		1,234.89

The other entry is not sales because these have already been accounted for as sales in an earlier accounting period.

Stage two

When inputting the opening trial balance the journal entry is:

	Dr £	Cr £
Assets (excluding Debtors)	3,345.67	
Suspense	1,234.89	
Liabilities		2,635.28
Capital		1,945.28
	4,580.56	4,580.56

Note how the suspense account entries cancel out to nil.

There is no VAT element in these opening invoices. The invoice should be recorded at the full amount and the VAT as £0.00. This is because the VAT has been accounted for in an earlier accounting period.

CONCLUSION

Remember to save your work and back up your disk if you wish to rework this exercise.

Printing reports

TYPES OF PRINTER

Let us look in more detail at using the printer. There are two types of printer which you might use:

- impact printers; and
- non-impact printers.

Impact printers

Daisywheel

The characters are moulded onto the ends of the petals of a small wheel (which is said to look like a daisy). The wheel spins round to position the correct character to be printed out. Additional characters can be added by using extra daisywheels. The printer cannot print graphics.

Some wheels spin in one direction only. Others spin in both directions to make printing quicker and more efficient.

Dot matrix

Each individual character is made up of dots selected from a grid of dots.

The dots are usually quite noticeable and the quality is therefore not acceptable for letters and reports.

Some people find it almost impossible to read. It is probably best used for financial reports which are really only kept as a copy of information stored within the system.

Some printers have an NLQ (or Near Letter Quality) function which prints each character twice slightly offset to increase the density of the print. These printers can be used to print graphics.

Non-impact printers

Laser

These printers produce very high quality characters and graphics. A laser is used to transfer the image (rather than individual characters) onto a drum which transfers the image to the paper.

A wide variety of fonts (styles of character) can be used.

Ink jet

Ink is sprayed onto the printing surface. This can be almost any surface including paper, plastic or metal.

The quality is excellent and can be used for both text and graphics.

USING THE PRINTER

Before using your printer (as with all electrical equipment), read the manual carefully. Look out for these procedures in particular:

- Connecting the printer to the computer.
- Switching the printer on.
- Checking that the printer is *on-line* (ie. ready to print).
- Aligning the paper.
- Advancing the paper to the top of the next page.
- Stopping the printer safely (eg. to unblock a paper jam).

Before you can print out your first report you will probably have to select the type of printer used from a list provided by the package.

The command to print will normally be part of the package you are using.

PRINTER PROBLEMS

When using the printer it can be frustrating when you have problems. Here are some of the more common problems with some of the possible reasons. This is not an exhaustive list and you should always read the manual before dealing with a fault.

Fault	*Reason*
Printer does not print out when command is given	printer not switched on
	printer not connected to computer
	printer not on-line
	wrong command used
Output is not as expected (eg. characters used, characters wrong size, spacing incorrect)	wrong printer type selected
	printer incompatible with software
	printer cable faulty
	printer using incorrect fonts
	fonts have not been downloaded correctly from computer to printer
Quality poor, characters faint	ribbon or cartridge needs replacing
Paper jam	wrong paper used
	paper damaged
Printed crooked on paper	paper not aligned properly

TYPES OF PAPER

The type of printer which you are using will dictate which type of paper you can use.

The two types of paper available are:

- continuous stationery; and
- single sheet paper.

Continuous stationery

This stationery tends to be a sandwich of several copies which are printed simultaneously. The paper feeds through as one continuous sheet with individual pages marked by perforations. The length of page must be set (usually through the software) so that the printer starts each page of text at the top of a new page of paper.

There tends to be a lot of handling required to prepare documents for distribution and filing. The paper sandwich is held together by side strips which have holes which fit over the sprockets on the printer. These strips must be torn off to separate the copies (decollating). The individual pages must also be separated for distribution (bursting).

This type of stationery is obviously suitable for producing multiple copies of documents such as delivery notes, invoices and purchase orders. For these standard documents the business would possibly have its own pre-printed stationery, although most accounting packages do have accompanying standard forms.

Some businesses also use computer cheques. These are supplied by the bank and are customised for the particular business. They tend to be used in conjunction with the creditors' ledger (and payroll) programs. Invoices for payment are identified and cheques are automatically produced during a cheque run. A remittance advice is usually printed at the same time.

Single sheet paper

This is usually placed in a special tray or feeder. The printer takes a fresh page as it requires one.

Distributing reports

Before distributing reports or any other printed documents you should check the quality carefully. This will save time in the long run because you will not have to answer any queries or re-print reports (and this may be impossible anyway).

Remember that when you send a report or document internally you should always include at least a compliments slip with your name and the identity of the report on it.

If the report is confidential put it in a suitable envelope, seal the envelope and mark it *private and confidential*.

When sending documents to customers or suppliers, follow the procedures of your organisation.

Recording and accounting for sales and debtors

PRODUCING SALES INVOICES

In the first case study, we looked at the inputting of manually produced invoices. We will now look at the debtors' ledger in more detail, in particular producing sales invoices.

We will also look in more detail at how sales are analysed.

We are going to look at Greensleeves Ltd again. Do not worry – we are not going to re-input all the standing data!

All you need is one customer account as follows:

Fred Brown & Associates
234 Barlow Moor Road
West Didsbury
Manchester
M19 5DG

Telephone: 0161 456 8833 Contact: Fred Brown

This is already set up as account number 000001.

You also need the following nominal ledger accounts.

4000	Sales A – men's
4001	Sales B – women's
4002	Sales C – children's
8100	Bad debt write-off
1100	Debtors control
2200	Tax control account (VAT)
9998	Suspense account

Note how the business has three different types of sales. These sales are different types of supply for VAT purposes.

Category	*Goods supplied*	*VAT rate*
1	Men's T-shirts	Standard
2	Women's T-shirts	Standard
3	Children's T-shirts	Zero

Standard rate is currently 17.5% and zero rate is 0%. (Do not confuse this with items which are exempt or outside of the scope of VAT.)

VAT RATES

You will probably have to set up the rates of VAT which are currently charged. This will probably include codes for exempt and outside of scope.

Which screen will you use to input these rates?

Question 1

Which transactions fall outside the scope of VAT?

SETTING UP PRODUCT CODES

To save typing out the items sold on each individual invoice you can set up a *product file*.

Identify the route to setting up/amending the product file.

Here are the products for you to input. These prices *exclude* VAT.

Check in your manual that product prices should be stated exclusive of VAT.

Stock Code	*Description*	*Unit of sale*	*Unit price £*	*VAT rate*
001	Green (men's)	Each	7.50	Standard
002	Blue (men's)	Each	7.50	Standard
003	Red (men's)	Each	7.50	Standard
004	Yellow (men's)	Each	7.50	Standard
005	Green (women's)	Each	6.50	Standard
006	Blue (women's)	Each	6.50	Standard
007	Red (women's)	Each	6.50	Standard
008	Yellow (women's)	Each	6.50	Standard
009	Green (children's)	Each	4.00	Zero
010	Blue (children's)	Each	4.00	Zero
011	Red (children's)	Each	4.00	Zero
012	Yellow (children's)	Each	4.00	Zero

Print out a *product list*. Record the commands here.

Before we can invoice customers you *may* have to put some goods into stock. We need to update opening stock. Record the commands here.

Enter as follows:

Stock code	*Description*	*Quantity*	*Cost*
002	Blue	5	£6
004	Yellow	10	£6
008	Yellow	5	£5
009	Green	5	£3.50
010	Blue	8	£3.50
007	Red	10	£5

Now go into the invoice generating option. Record the commands here.

You are required to invoice Fred Brown & Associates (account number 1) as follows.

Date	As per system		
Invoice no.	1		
Order no.	23		
Discount rate	0% or ignore		
Product no.	002	008	009
Quantity	3	4	5

Make sure you allocate each sale to the correct nominal code (as above).

Now print out the invoice. Record the commands here.

Question 2

What is the double-entry to record this sale?

Sage House
Benton Park Road
Newcastle Upon Tyne
NE7 7LZ

Tel: 0191 201 0308
VAT No: 357 0469 41

Fred Brown Associates
234 Barlow Moor Rd
West Didsbury
Manchester
M19 5DG

INVOICE

INVOICE	1
DATE/TAX POINT	*
ORDER	23
ACCOUNT NO.	000001

QUANTITY	DETAILS	DISC	NET PRICE	VAT
3.00	Blue (men's)	0.00	22.50	3.94
4.00	Yellow (women's)	0.00	26.00	4.55
5.00	Green (children's)	0.00	20.00	0.00

... AS INVOICED ...

NET	68.50
VAT	8.49
CARRIAGE	0.00
TOTAL	76.99

View Fred Brown's transaction history on screen. It should look like this. The unpaid items are marked with a star.

Sage Educational	Transaction History

A/C Ref. :	000001	Balance:	93.39
A/C Name:	FRED BROWN ASSOCIATES	Amount paid:	44.40
Credit limit:	1000.00	Turnover:	121.06

No.	*Tp*	*Date*	*Ref*	*Details*	*Value*	*Debit*	*Credit*
23	SI	040693	7		45.17	45.17	
27	SD	040693		Discount	0.77		0.77
28	SR	040693		Sales receipt	44.40		44.40
48	SI	070693	1	Blue (men's)	26.44*		
49	SI	070693	1	Yellow (women's)	30.55*		
50	SI	070693	1	Green (children's)	20.00*	76.99	

	Future	Current	30 Days	60 Days	90 Days	Older
Aged:	0.00	76.99	0.00	0.00	0.00	

OFFERING SETTLEMENT DISCOUNTS

Let us now offer Fred Brown & Associates a 2% discount if he settles his invoices within 10 days.

Where will you set up this discount?

Check in your manual if you can set this up in the customer details or if the discount must be specified on each invoice.

Now generate the following invoice.

Date	As per system	
Invoice no.	2	
Order no.	24	
Discount rate	2% 10 days	
Product no.	002	008
Quantity	1	1

Before printing out the invoice, calculate the amount of VAT which will be charged at each rate.

Sage House
Benton Park Road
Newcastle Upon Tyne
NE7 7LZ

Tel: 0191 201 0308
VAT No: 357 0469 41

Fred Brown Associates
234 Barlow Moor Rd
West Didsbury
Manchester
M19 5DG

INVOICE

INVOICE	2
DATE/TAX POINT	*
ORDER	24
ACCOUNT NO.	000001

QUANTITY	DETAILS	DISC	NET PRICE	VAT
1.00	Blue (men's)	0.00	7.50	1.29
1.00	Yellow (women's)	0.00	6.50	1.11

... AS INVOICED ...

Discount of £0.28 may be deducted for payment in 10 days

NET	14.00
VAT	2.40
CARRIAGE	0.00
TOTAL	16.40

Question 3

What is the double entry to record this sale?

Print the invoice (as before).

We also need to post these invoices to the ledger. Record the command here.

PRINTING THE AGED DEBTORS' REPORT

Now run the month-end procedure. We will assume that we are now moving into the next month. You will have to exit the program and change the *run date* (*or actual date*) to one month later than the actual date. Generate the following invoice to Fred Brown Associates.

Date	As per system		
Invoice no.	3		
Order no.	25		
Discount rate	2% 10 days		
Product no.	004	007	010
Quantity	10	3	2

Now print out the *aged debtors' report* (or *listing*). Record the commands here.

Sales Ledger – Account Balances (Aged)

A/C	*Account name*	*Turnover*	*Credit limit*	*Balance*	*Current*	*30 days*	*60 days*	*90 days*	*Older*
000001	Fred Brown Associates Fred Brown (0161 456 8833)	223.56	1000.00	212.09	118.70	93.39	0.00	0.00	0.00
	Totals	223.56	1000.00	212.09	118.70	93.39	0.00	0.00	0.00

Sage House
Benton Park Road
Newcastle Upon Tyne
NE7 7LZ

Tel: 0191 201 0308
VAT No: 357 0469 41

Fred Brown Associates
234 Barlow Moor Rd
West Didsbury
Manchester
M19 5DG

INVOICE

INVOICE	3
DATE/TAX POINT	*
ORDER	25
ACCOUNT NO.	000001

QUANTITY	DETAILS	DISC	NET PRICE	VAT
10.00	Yellow (men's)	0.00	75.00	12.86
3.00	Red (women's)	0.00	19.50	3.34
2.00	Blue (children's)	0.00	8.00	0.00

... AS INVOICED ...

Discount of £2.05 may be deducted for payment within 10 days

NET	102.50
VAT	16.20
CARRIAGE	0.00
TOTAL	118.70

PRINTING OUT STATEMENTS OF ACCOUNT

Once you are satisfied that the ageing is correct, you can then print out the statement of account to send to the customer. These are essentially the same as the ledger accounts, but you would print them on special stationery to make them look more professional.

What are the commands for printing out statements?

STATEMENT

Fred Brown Associates
234 Barlow Moor Road
West Didsbury
Manchester
M19 5DG

A/C Ref	000001
Date	*
Page	1

Date	Ref	Details	Debit	Credit
*	1	Blue (men's)		
*	1	Yellow (women's)		
*	1	Green (children's)	76.99	
*	2	Blue (men's)		
*	2	Yellow (women's)	16.40	
*	3	Yellow (men's)		
*	3	Red (women's)		
*	3	Blue (children's)	118.70	

Current	30 Day	60 Day	90 Day	120+ Day
118.80	93.39	0.00	0.00	0.00

Amount due **212.09**

REMITTANCE ADVICE

Fred Brown Associates
234 Barlow Moor Road
West Didsbury
Manchester
M19 5DG

A/C Ref	000001
Date	*
Page	1

Date	Ref	Details	Debit	Credit
*	1	Blue		
*	1	Yellow		
*	1	Green	76.99	
*	2	Blue		
*	2	Yellow	16.40	
*	3	Yellow		
*	3	Red		
*	3	Blue	118.70	

Amount due **212.09**

POSTING CREDIT NOTES

As with invoices, there are usually two methods of posting credit notes. These are:

- generating the credit notes by using the option within the program; or
- inputting manual (ie. generated by some other means) credit notes.

Generate the following credit note for Fred Brown & Associates to refund the customer for an item on invoice no. 1 which was faulty.

Date	As per system
Credit note no.	4
Product no.	008
Quantity	4

Remember to use the F9 (Footing) function to discount the VAT.

Sage House
Benton Park Road
Newcastle Upon Tyne
NE7 7LZ

Tel: 0191 201 0308
VAT No: 357 0469 41

Fred Brown Associates
234 Barlow Moor Rd
West Didsbury
Manchester
M19 5DG

INVOICE (CREDIT)

INVOICE	4
DATE/TAX POINT	*
ORDER	0
ACCOUNT NO.	000001

QUANTITY	DETAILS	DISC	NET PRICE	VAT
4.00	Yellow (women's)	0.00	26.00	4.46

... AS INVOICED ...

NET	26.00
VAT	4.46
CARRIAGE	0.00
TOTAL	30.46

Make sure you remembered to discount the VAT because the original invoice offered a settlement discount.

If you display the individual ledger account the credit note will appear as a *negative entry*.

Obviously this credit note relates to one particular invoice and you will want to *allocate* it against that invoice. The method of allocating will depend upon the package you are using. See the *manual* for the *exact* procedure.

> ***Question 4***
>
> *What is the double-entry to record this credit note?*

BAD DEBTS

Bad debts must be written off within the *debtor's ledger* if the debt clearly cannot be recovered.

The amount owed is cancelled by issuing a credit note, or the package may have a special notice. Let us say we want to write off invoice 3 which we now have to admit will not be paid. The original invoice totalled £118.70, including VAT of £16.20

> ***Question 5***
>
> *What is the double-entry to record the write-off of this bad debt?*

Note that the VAT and sales accounts in the nominal ledger are unaffected by the write-off.

The VAT account is unaffected because the company *cannot* reclaim the VAT unless the customer has gone into liquidation. If this is so then the company must fill out certain forms and receive permission from HM Customs & Excise.

If you are using a credit note to write off bad debts, it must be allocated against the bad debt nominal ledger account code, *not* sales.

If you are using an automatic bad debt routine, the system will post the entries to the correct accounts for you.

CONTRA ENTRIES

Let us look at an example. Let us assume that Fred Brown & Associates are also suppliers of the company. The following balances are to be found in the ledgers.

	£
Debtor's ledger	345.66
Creditors' ledger	234.55

> ***Question 6***
>
> *What is the double-entry to perform a contra entry between the two accounts?*

Note that this is always the double entry for a contra entry. This double entry is unlikely, however, to be possible if you are using a ledger package. As the debtors' and creditors' ledgers are essentially separate modules, a special procedure is needed to deal with contras.

You will need an extra nominal ledger account called *contras* (code 9998); you can use *suspense*.

To make the contra entry issue a credit note in the debtors' ledger module and record a credit note in the creditors' ledger module.

In both cases the *nominal ledger account* is *contras* (9998). There is no effect on the VAT control account.

Question 7

What is the double-entry effect of posting these two credit notes?

Recording and accounting for purchases and creditors

VAT RATES

You will probably have to set up the rates of VAT which are currently charged.

Question 1

Which codes will you need to set up for VAT?

Which screen will you use to input these rates?

RECORDING PURCHASE INVOICES

We will now move on to the recording of purchase invoices. This is essentially the mirror image of recording sales invoices.

Use the following supplier accounts (set up in the previous exercise).

Trevor Manufacturing Ltd
345 Taylforth Road
Sale
Manchester
M24 2KN

Telephone:	0161 345 2234	Contact:	Harold Goodman

Olympic Design Studio
34 Weaver Street
Withington
Manchester
M20 2JL

Telephone:	0161 404 4654	Contact:	Betty Davies

You will also need the following nominal ledger codes.

5001	Purchases A – Men's
5002	Purchases B – Women's
5003	Purchases C – Children's
2200	Tax control account (VAT)
2100	Creditors control account
9998	Contras

Purchase invoices should be stamped with a consecutive number and recorded on receipt in a *purchase invoice register*. They should only be recorded in the creditors' ledger once they have been coded and authorised.

Now identify the commands for recording purchase invoices.

Here are some invoices for you to input. (You are using the purchase invoice register as your source.)

Invoice No.	*Supplier*	*Nominal code*	*Total* £	*VAT* £	*Net* £
1	Olympic Design Studio	5002	267.89	39.90	227.99
2	Trevor Manufacturing	5003	111.92	–	111.92
3	Olympic Design Studio	5001	178.99	26.66	152.33

Print (or view) the ledger accounts for these two suppliers.

Question 2

What is the double-entry to record these purchase invoices?

POSTING CREDIT NOTES

Identify the commands to post credit notes.

Here is a credit note for you to post.

CN No.	*Supplier*	*Nominal code*	*Total* £	*VAT* £	*Net* £
1	Olympic Design Studio	2	30.02	4.47	25.55

Remember to allocate the credit note to the same VAT code and nominal ledger code as the original invoice.

CONTRA ENTRIES

We have already seen the procedure for dealing with contra entries above.

Question 3

What is the procedure for making contra entries?

Question 4

To which VAT code should contra entries be posted?

Making period-end adjustments

NOMINAL CODES

You will need the following codes for this session:

Office equipment	0030
O/E depreciation	0031
Accruals	2109
Prepayments	1103
Rent	7100
Consultancy fees	7602
Office equipment depreciation	8004

ACCRUALS AND PREPAYMENTS

During the previous session you exited the system and changed the run date in order to practise using the aged debtors report.

Exit the system again, but this time log in using today's date.

Question 1

Your company has just paid a year's rent of £1,380 in advance. This must be shown as a prepayment.

First of all enter the cash payment and code it to 7100 (rent).

What is the double entry to reflect a month-end prepayment?

Question 2

How would you charge one month's rent to the profit and loss account?

To make the prepayment entry you may be able to use an automatic prepayment/accruals function or you may have to process the adjustments via individual journals.

Which does your chosen program offer? How does it work?

An automatic prepayment journal automatically calculates the amount to be charged to the P&L each month. These P&L charges are only posted to the ledgers when the month end options are run.

Accruals work in a similar way.

The company is hiring some consultants for the next three months. The charges for this service will be built up over the next three months and the total of £360 will not be paid until the end of the period. Process these adjustments.

Now print out a month-end report to confirm the postings and view the accounts concerned so you can see the transactions history.

They should appear as shown on the following pages.

Sage Educational	Transaction History	Date 08/06/95

A/C Ref 1103 **Control N/C** A/C Name Prepayments

No.	Tp	Date	Ref	Details	Value	Debit	Credit
59	JD	08/06/93	Prepay rent		1380.00	1380.00	
61	JC	08/06/93	Prepay rent		115.00		115.00

	Debit	Credit
Totals	1380.00	115.00
Balance	1265.00	

A/C Ref 2109 **Control N/C** A/C Name Accruals

No.	Tp	Date	Ref	Details	Value	Debit	Credit
63	JC	08/06/93	Accrue consultancy		1200.00		1200.00

	Debit	Credit
Totals	0.00	1200.00
Balance	0.00	1200.00

A/C Ref 7100 Control N/C A/C Name Rent

No.	Tp	Date	Ref	Details	Value	Debit	Credit
57	BP	08/06/93		1 yr rent	1380.00	1380.00	
58	JC	08/06/93	Prepay rent		1380.00		1380.00
60	JC	08/06/93	Prepay rent		115.00	115.00	

	Debit	Credit
Totals	1495.00	1380.00
Balance	115.00	

A/C Ref 7602 A/C Name Consultancy fees

No.	Tp	Date	Ref	Details	Value	Debit	Credit
62	JD	08/06/93	Accrue consultancy		120.00	120.00	

	Debit	Credit
Totals	120.00	0.00
Balance	120.00	

DEPRECIATION

The company has purchased a new computer for cash:

	£
Supply and installation	4,000
VAT	700
Total	4,700

Enter the transaction as usual.

It has been decided to depreciate the computer on a straight-line basis over four years.

Question 3

What is the annual depreciation charge?

Question 4

What is the double-entry for one month's depreciation charge?

If your package does not have an automatic journal function you would have to input each month's depreciation via a separate journal. However most packages do have an automatic system.

Describe your system's depreciation routine.

Enter the depreciation journal and run the month-end report. View your transactions on the screen.

PREPARING VAT RETURNS

VAT returns

VAT (Value Added Tax) returns are usually made every quarter. The business must then pay the VAT owed to Customs, unless the tax control account has a debit balance – in which case a refund is claimed.

The VAT return requires analysis of sales and purchases into standard-rated, zero-rated and exempt.

How does your package achieve this?

Recording and accounting for payroll

INTRODUCTION

The following instructions relate to Sage Sterling Payroll 1995/96. Tax and other rates used are those for the year 6 April 1995 to 5 April 1996.

All tax charges calculated assume that lower rate tax relief is available (20% on the first £3,200 of taxable income). The exercises in this Study Pack assume the 1995/96 rates apply in all cases.

Installation of payroll package

These instructions assume that you have already loaded another Sage Accounting package (eg. **Accountant Plus**). Ensure you have sufficient memory to load the whole package; you will need a minimum of 1.5 megabytes plus extra memory for employee details.

Switch on and at **C:>** prompt

Type A:	then press **return**
Type INSTALL	then press **return**

Follow instructions on screen; you will see all the software files being loaded. Once all files are in the memory, the installation program will tell you it has completed the task and you know all the files are complete.

Running software

To run software at **C:>** prompt

Type CD Sage	then press **return**
Type Sage	then press **return**

Password

See Sage manual or Financial Training Study Planner.

Select **Payroll** from main menu.

INPUTTING COMPANY DETAILS

This case study looks once again at Greensleeves Ltd. The Sage Educational package, however, will not display any company name other than Sage.

For these exercises we will be using the 1995/96 tax calendar for putting the information onto Sage and entering the date manually at the beginning of each payroll run, starting at 28.4.95. This should be week 4, month 1.

Read the introduction to your manual carefully and then look through the rest of the manual quickly to identify the options available.

Make sure you identify any special uses of the keys.

Company details and information

Here are the payroll details for *Greensleeves Ltd*. To input the data go through the menu screens as indicated in **bold** print.

Company details
Company information

Company name	Greensleeves Ltd
Address	123 Greenwood Road Withington Manchester M20 4TF
Bank name	Southern Bank plc
Branch	10 High Street, Withington
Sort code	22–11–58
Account name	Payroll account
Account number	90239151
Tax office reference	345/6789
Rounding indicator	0.00

Press **Esc** to return to Company Details menu. Now we will input the different ways of paying the Greensleeve employees. Employees are paid on a monthly or hourly basis. Overtime is also paid and bonuses are given to some employees. This is input as follows:

Payment types

1	Monthly basic
2	Hourly basic
3	O/time – hours

Leave all the columns at their default of 'Y' (ie. Yes).

Press **Esc** to return to Company Details menu.

Adjustment types

1	Bonus

Again, leave all the other figures at their default settings.

Press **Esc** twice to return to main menu.

BASIC EMPLOYEE RECORDS

Now that we have set up the basic company details we can set up the records of some of Greensleeves' employees.

To input basic employee records

We will look at two employees, one of whom is paid monthly, the other weekly. To input the data you go through the menu as follows:

Employee details
Add a new employee

Employee 1

Note how the screen has given you a blank pro forma to fill in. At the moment it says 'Unused employee' in the surname slot. As you fill in the following details, this will be overwritten. Now type in the following, remembering to press the 'enter' button at the end of each entry you make.

Screen 1

Employee number	1
First name	Jane
Surname	Howard
Address	567 Whitchurch Road
	Withington
	Manchester
	M20 1XX
Works number	1
Payment type	QM (cheque monthly)
Pension ref	0
Auto SSP/SMP	Y
Birth date	05/04/63
Join date	12/12/90
Tax code	300L
Tax basis	Normal cumulative
Effective from	6.4.95
NI number	WS 27 84 33 J
NI category	A
Marital status	M
Director	No

Screen 2

Department code	2
Qualifying days	5
Rates of pay	1 (Pressing 1 [return] automatically brings up the payment type), then enter 1000 in the third column.
Adjustments	1 (This also automatically types in 'Bonus' for you as prescribed by he information typed in previously under company details.)

Screen 3

Allows you to enter attachment of earnings information if it is applicable. Ignore this screen by pressing **enter** to pass on to screen 4.

Screen 4

Banking information	Not applicable
Previous employment	Not applicable
Current employment	
Gross pay for NI	Not applicable
Rounding c/f	Not applicable

Screen 5 onwards Not applicable

Jane is paid £1,000 a month. She is paid by cheque (so no bank information is relevant).

Press **F10** to move to next employee.

Employee 2

Screen 1

First name	Kevin
Surname	Baker
Address	28 Bard Road Withington Manchester M20 3YY
Works number	2
Payment type	CW (cash weekly)
Pension ref	0
Auto SSP/SMP	Y
Birth date	20/9/67
Join date	19/5/88
Tax code	250L
Effective from	6.4.95
NI number	TR 23 18 85 H
NI category	A
Marital status	S
Director	No

Screen 2

Department code	1
Qualifying days	5
Rates of pay	2 (Pressing 2 [return] automatically brings up the payment type), then enter 5.048 in the third column. 3 O/time – hours: 10.096 (Double time)
Adjustments	1

Note that Kevin is paid in cash weekly, based on a standard week of 40 hours at an hourly rate of £5.048, with double time for overtime.

Screen 3

Again this relates to attachment of earnings and can be ignored.

Screen 4

Banking information	Not applicable
Previous employment	Not applicable
Current employment	
Gross pay for NI	605 (You must always enter total NI earnings to date if you are starting to computerise payroll part-way through the tax year.)
Rounding c/f	Not applicable

Let us assume it is week 4 in the *income tax* calendar. This means that Kevin has already been paid three times this tax year (£605.76).

Screen 5

You will have to input the following *brought forward* figures, ie. the cumulative figures so far this tax year. (Remember this is all for this employment.)

Total gross pay	605.76
Taxable gross pay	605.76
Tax paid	106.01
Standard NI earnings	£605
NI contributions to date	Employee – £46.53 Employer – £42.30

Press **Esc** to return to menu.

Note: The action prompt appears on the screen – you want to 'post' the information just entered. If you need help, press the F1 function key; pressing Esc will clear the help window off the screen.

Let us assume that in the first week/month these employees are going to be paid their basic rate *only*; that is, no overtime or other variations.

PROCESSING THE PAYROLL

The SAGE Payroll 2 system has pre-set 52 tax weeks and 12 tax months based on the year 6 April to 5 April.

As a result, to process week 1 you must enter a run day between **6 April** and **12 April**. To process the payroll for month 1 you must enter a date between **6 April** and **3 May.**

To process week 4 and month 1, the payroll run date should be set as **28 April**, with each run advancing one week or month as appropriate.

Only the weekly payroll should be processed each week whilst the monthly payroll should be processed every 4 or 5 weeks.

We will now run the payroll for Greensleeves for week 4, month 1 and produce a payslip for both employees.

Processing payroll	Follow instructions on screen. You will have to do weekly payments in a separate run to monthly payments.
Enter payments	Enter the appropriate number of *units* of basic pay. This will interact with employee details to calculate gross pay, tax and NICs. For Jane, you enter 1 in the first box (for one month's work). Foe Kevin you enter 40 (number of hours worked).
F10	To select next employee
Esc	To return to Processing payroll menu
Payment summary	To check figures prior to printing other reports

Printing out payslips

Processing payroll
Payslips

Print out the *payslips* – firstly for the weekly employee Kevin, then repeat with the processing selected for 'monthly' employees to run the programme for Jane Howard.

Note that for most systems you must keep an *extra* copy of the payslip as a *substitute* P11 (*deductions working sheet*).

PAYSLIP

		RATE	GROSS PAY	DEDUCTIONS		CUMULATIVES	
Monthly basic:	1.0000	1000.0000	1000.00	PAYE Tax	173.91	Total gross pay TD	1000.00
	–	–	–	National Ins.	80.04	Gross for tax TD	1000.00
	–	–	–	Pension	–	Tax paid TD	173.91
	–	–	–		–	Earnings for NI TD	1000.00
Bonus:	–	–	–		–	National Ins. TD	80.04
	–	–	–		–	Pension TD	–
					–		
Sick pay	–	–	–		–	Earnings for NI	1000.00
Maternity pay	–	–	–	Rounding b/f	–	Gross for tax	1000.00
Holiday pay	–	–	–	Rounding c/f	–	TOTAL GROSS PAY	1000.00
						National Ins Number	WS278433J

1	28/04/95	2	QM	300L	1	JANE HOWARD	Net pay
Month	Date	Dept	Payment	Tax code	Employee ref		£746.05

PAYSLIP

		RATE	GROSS PAY	DEDUCTIONS		CUMULATIVES	
Hourly basic:	40.0000	5.0480	201.92	PAYE Tax	35.18	Total gross pay TD	807.68
Overtime hours:	–	10.0960	–	National Ins.	15.51	Gross for tax TD	807.68
	–	–	–	Pension	–	Tax paid TD	141.19
	–	–	–		–	Earnings for NI TD	806.00
Bonus:	–	–	–		–	National Ins. TD	62.04
	–	–	–		–	Pension TD	–
					–		
Sick pay	–	–	–		–	Earnings for NI	201.00
Maternity pay	–	–	–	Rounding b/f	–	Gross for tax	201.92
Holiday pay	–	–	–	Rounding c/f	–	TOTAL GROSS PAY	201.92
						National Ins Number	TR231885H

4	28/04/95	1	CW	250L	2	KEVIN BAKER	Net pay
Week	Date	Dept	Payment	Tax code	Employee ref		£151.23

Printing cheques

Processing payroll
Print cheques (with special stationery you can print out smart cheques incorporating logos and designs)

Printing the cash analysis report

Processing payroll
Cash analysis

Cash analysis Date: 28/04/95

Tax (Week 04, Month 01) Page: 1

Ref	*Employee name*	*Net pay*	*£50*	*£20*	*£10*	*£5*	*£1*	*50p*	*20p*	*10p*	*5p*	*2p*	*1p*	*Totals*
2	K Baker	151.23	3	0	0	0	1	0	1	0	0	1	1	
	Quantities		3	0	0	0	1	0	1	0	0	1	1	
	Values		150.00	0.00	0.00	0.00	1.00	0.00	0.20	0.00	0.00	0.02	0.01	151.23

Printing the payroll summary

Processing payroll
Payment summary

Print out the payroll summaries (weekly and monthly). You may be able to do this by department as well as for the company as a whole.

You will need to study the manual carefully to find out which reports are available and which you *must* print out.

For instance you must have a report which summarises payroll totals. You need this to prepare the *journal entry* to record the payroll charge in the nominal ledger.

You must also have a report which summarises the amount owed to the Collector of Taxes under the PAYE system.

> ***Question 1***
>
> *Which amounts must be paid over to the Collector of Taxes?*

PAYMENTS SUMMARY – PART 1
Monthly

Date: 28/04/95
Page: 1

Ref.	Total gross pay	Taxable gross pay	Pre-tax Addition	Pre-tax Deduct'n	Pension	PAYE	Nat. Ins.	SSP	SMP	Post-tax Addition	Post-tax Deduct'n	Amount B/F	Amount C/F	Net pay
1	1000.00	1000.00	0.00	0.00	0.00	173.91	80.04	0.00	0.00	0.00	0.00	0.00	0.00	746.05
1 employee	1000.00	1000.00	0.00	0.00	0.00	173.91	80.04	0.00	0.00	0.00	0.00	0.00	0.00	746.05

PAYMENTS SUMMARY – PART 2
National Insurance

Ref.	Name	Standard earnings	Total contribution	Employees contribution	Con/out earnings	Con/Out contribution	Employers Nat. Ins.	Employers Pension	Tax code	Nat. Ins. category
1	J Howard	1000.00	182.24	80.04	0.00	0.00	102.20	0.00	300L	A
Total values for 1 employee		1000.00	182.24	80.04	0.00	0.00	102.20	0.00		

PAYMENTS SUMMARY – PART 3
Year to date

Ref.	Name	Total gross pay	Taxable gross pay	PAYE	National Insurance Employees	National Insurance Employers	SSP	SMP	Pension Employee	Pension Employer
1	J Howard	1000.00	1000.00	173.91	80.04	102.20	0.00	0.00	0.00	0.00
Total values for 1 employee		1000.00	1000.00	173.91	80.04	102.20	0.00	0.00	0.00	0.00

PAYMENTS SUMMARY – PART 1
Weekly

Date: 28/04/95
Page: 1

Ref.	Total gross pay	Taxable gross pay	Pre-tax Addition	Pre-tax Deduct'n	Pension	PAYE	Nat. Ins.	SSP	SMP	Post-tax Addition	Post-tax Deduct'n	Amount B/F	Amount C/F	Net pay
2	201.92	201.92	0.00	0.00	0.00	35.18	15.51	0.00	0.00	0.00	0.00	0.00	0.00	151.23
1 employee	201.92	201.92	0.00	0.00		35.18	15.51	0.00	0.00	0.00	0.00	0.00	0.00	151.23

PAYMENTS SUMMARY – PART 2
National Insurance

Ref.	Name	Standard earnings	Total contribution	Employees contribution	Con/out earnings	Con/Out contribution	Employers Nat. Ins.	Employers Pension	Tax code	Nat. Ins. category
2	K Baker	201.00	29.61	15.51	0.00	0.00	14.10	0.00	250L	A
Total values for 1 employee		201.00	29.61	15.51	0.00	0.00	14.10	0.00		–

PAYMENTS SUMMARY – PART 3
Year to date

Ref.	Name	Total gross pay	Taxable gross pay	PAYE	National Insurance Employees	National Insurance Employers	SSP	SMP	Pension Employee	Pension Employer
2	K Baker	807.68	807.68	141.19	62.04	56.40	0.00	0.00	0.00	0.00
Total values for 1 employee		807.68	807.68	141.19	62.04	56.40	0.00	0.00	0.00	0.00

CLOSING OFF THE PAYROLL PERIOD

Once you are certain that the payroll has been completed correctly and you have printed out all the reports you need, you must close off the payroll period by updating the records. This is a vital process; if you fail to update the records, the cumulative totals are incorrectly stated in subsequent periods and so tax and NICs will be incorrectly calculated.

The commands to do this are as follows:

Processing payroll
Update records — Follow the instructions. The computer will inform you as to how many employees in which payment category have been updated.

Then you can proceed in the knowledge that this month's/week's processing is saved. Remember to update both monthly and weekly employees – as this has to be done separately.

Printing the PAYE remittance report

Processing payroll
P32 Payment Record

Employer's Payment Record (Form P32) Date: 28/04/95

(1) Total SSP	*(2) SSP Recovered*	*(3) SMP*	*(4) NIC Comp'n*	*(5) Total Ded.*	*(6) Gross NI*	*(7) Net NI*	*(8) PAYE Tax*	*(9) Total Due*
0.00	0.00	0.00	0.00	0.00	211.85	211.85	209.09	420.94

NIC compensation percentage	Employee range	Data range
SMP: 4.00	0001 - 0005	Week: 060495 – 280495 Month: 060495 – 280495

At this point, save your work to floppy disk, quit Sage and return to the DOS prompt.

Re-enter the Sage payroll using the following week's date (ie. 31 May 1995).

VARIATIONS ON GROSS PAY

Your package will probably have standard types of pay already programmed into it.

> ***Question 2***
>
> *Name some elements which go to make up gross pay.*

Let us look at the effect on gross pay of these elements.

We are only going to process the weekly pay in week 5. Let us assume that Kevin is to receive the following payment in addition to his basic pay.

Overtime — 5 hours at double time (twice normal rate)

Now run the payroll processing routine identified earlier. To check the results of the processing, print out the payslip. (Normally you would print out all the reports if this were a proper payroll run.)

PAYSLIP

		RATE	GROSS PAY	DEDUCTIONS		CUMULATIVES	
Hourly basic:	40.0000	5.0480	201.92	PAYE Tax	47.92	Total gross pay TD	1060.08
Overtime hours:	5.0000	10.0960	50.48	National Ins.	20.61	Gross for tax TD	1060.08
	-	-	-	Pension	-	Tax paid TD	189.11
	-	-	-		-	Earnings for NI TD	1058.00
Bonus:	-	-	-		-	National Ins. TD	82.65
	-	-	-		-	Pension TD	-
					-		
Sick pay	-	-	-		-	Earnings for NI	252.00
Maternity pay	-	-	-	Rounding b/f	-	Gross for tax	252.40
Holiday pay	-	-	-	Rounding c/f	-	TOTAL GROSS PAY	252.40
						National Ins Number	TR231885H

5	05/05/95	1	CW	250L	2	KEVIN BAKER	Net pay
Week	Date	Dept	Payment	Tax code	Employee ref		£183.87

When you are satisfied with the results, run the **update** records for Kevin and quit Sage.

HOLIDAY PAY

In week 6 (12th May), let us assume that Kevin is entitled to holiday pay. He is to be paid the following amounts in addition to his basic pay.

Holiday pay	2 weeks at basic rate (based on 40-hour week)
Bonus	£50.00

Remember that the employee is entitled to the pay as if he had been paid in the *latest* week of his holiday. For Kevin this is week 8. This will mean advancing the payroll process by *two weeks* for Kevin alone.

To enter holiday pay

Processing payroll Run date 12/05/95 (week 6)
Enter payments

Enter normal weekly basic hours.
Move down the screen to highlight **Total holiday pay**

Press **F3** – this menu will calculate holiday pay automatically and enter:

2 Periods to advance relating to 2 weeks

Press **return** twice and enter in the holiday pay routine.

80 basic hours (2 weeks holiday pay @ 40 hours per week)

Press **Esc** twice – you are now back at the main payments card with correct calculations of PAYE and NICs.

To input bonus payments

Bonus

Second screen. Insert £50 where indicated.

Run the payroll processing routine, print out the payslip and run the payroll update routines.

PAYSLIP

		RATE	GROSS PAY	DEDUCTIONS		CUMULATIVES	
Hourly rate:	40.0000	5.0480	201.92	PAYE Tax	118.52	Total gross pay TD	1715.84
Overtime hours:		10.0960		National Ins.	51.53	Gross for tax TD	1715.84
	–	–	–	Pension	–	Tax paid TD	307.63
	–	–	–		–	Earnings for NI TD	1711.00
Bonus	–	–	50.00		–	National Ins. TD	134.18
	–	–	–		–	Pension TD	–
					–		
Sick pay	–	–	–		–	Earnings for NI	653.00
Maternity pay	–	–	–	Rounding b/f	–	Gross for tax	655.76
Holiday pay	–	–	403.84	Rounding c/f	–	TOTAL GROSS PAY	655.76
						National Ins Number	TR231885H

6	12/05/95	1	CW	250L	2	KEVIN BAKER	Net pay
Week	Date	Dept	Payment	Tax code	Employee ref		£485.71

Now run the weekly payroll for:

Week 7 (19/05/95)
Week 8 (26/05/95)

The system will not allow you to input payment details for Kevin because he is on holiday.

Update the payroll for each week that you run, ie. for weeks 7 and 8.

Now you can view Kevin's P11 using:

Employee details
P11 Deduction Card (PAYE)

This will show that his pay for weeks 7 and 8 has been included automatically in the correct weeks.

In week 8 (26th May) Jane is also going to be paid, so set the payroll processing to monthly and process as usual, paying Jane £1,000. Print out her payslip.

Remember to update both categories of payment at the month-/week-end.

PAYSLIP

		RATE	GROSS PAY	DEDUCTIONS		CUMULATIVES	
Monthly basic:	1.0000	1000.0000	1000.00	PAYE Tax	173.92	Total gross pay TD	2000.00
	-	-	-	National Ins.	80.04	Gross for tax TD	2000.00
	-	-	-	Pension	-	Tax paid TD	347.83
	-	-	-		-	Earnings for NI TD	2000.00
Bonus:	-	-	-		-	National Ins. TD	160.68
	-	-	-		-	Pension TD	-
					-		
Sick pay	-	-	-		-	Earnings for NI	1000.00
Maternity pay	-	-	-	Rounding b/f	-	Gross for tax	1000.00
Holiday pay	-	-	-	Rounding c/f	-	TOTAL GROSS PAY	1000.00
						National Ins Number	WS278433J

2	26/05/95	2	QM	300L	1	JANE HOWARD	Net pay
Month	Date	Dept	Payment	Tax code	Employee ref		£746.04

OTHER DEDUCTIONS FROM PAY

So far we have looked at various elements of gross pay. Now let us look at different types of deductions.

The first thing to establish is the effect on the employee's income tax liability of making these deductions.

Question 3

Which deductions might be made from an employee's pay, other than tax and National Insurance?

Question 4

Which of these can be deducted before calculating the employee's tax liability?

Let us return to Kevin and assume that in week 9 (30th June) he works his normal 40 hours, but that he has decided to contribute £5.00 a week to his favourite charity and to save £6.00 a week under the company's SAYE scheme (which is linked to the employee share option scheme operated by the company) every week from now on.

The company details must be adjusted to allow for other deductions.

Company details
Adjustment types

2	GAYE
3	SAYE

Both GAYE and SAYE are deductions before tax, but not NICs or pension, so the supporting columns should show:

+/-	Tax	NI	Pen
–	Y	N	N

Return to the main menu and alter the employee details for the two adjustments (see **Setting up basic employee records**).

Process the weekly payroll as before ensuring the two adjustments are included on screen 2 of the payment card. The payroll run date will be 02/06/95 (week 9).

Notice how, for the first time, the gross pay to date is *not* the same as the gross *taxable* to date. The difference is the £11.00 deductions made before calculating income tax.

Update the records as usual.

PAYSLIP

		RATE	GROSS PAY	DEDUCTIONS		CUMULATIVES	
Hourly basic:	40.0000	5.0480	201.92	PAYE Tax	32.67	Total gross pay TD	1917.76
Overtime hours:	–	10.0960	–	National Ins.	15.51	Gross for tax TD	1906.76
	–	–	–	Pension	–	Tax paid TD	340.30
Bonus:	–	–			–	Earnings for NI TD	1912.00
GAYE:	–	–	5.00		–	National Ins. TD	149.69
SAYE:	–	–	6.00		–	Pension TD	–
					–		
Sick pay	–	–	–		–	Earnings for NI	201.00
Maternity pay	–	–	–	Rounding b/f	–	Gross for tax	190.92
Holiday pay	–	–	–	Rounding c/f	–	TOTAL GROSS PAY	201.92
						National Ins Number	TR231885H

9	02/06/95	1	CW	250L	2		Net pay
Week	Date	Dept	Payment	Tax code	Employee ref	KEVIN BAKER	£142.74

SUPERANNUATION PAYMENTS

Let us assume that in week 10 Kevin is invited to join the pension scheme. His employer runs an *occupational pension scheme* which is approved by the Inland Revenue.

The scheme is a COMP *scheme* (Contacted-Out Money Purchase).

Kevin pays 2% on all earnings (including overtime, bonus etc.) and his employer pays 3% (on the same basis).

You will also have to amend Kevin's NI code to D as the COMP scheme is contracted out of SERPS (State Earnings Related Pension Scheme).

To set up the scheme within the company

Company details
Pension schemes

The first entry in the pension schemes should be:

Employer rate	3%
Reb	Y
Tot	N
Lim	N
Employee rate	2%
Reb	Y
Tot	N
Lim	N
Scon reference	123456Z
Tax relief	Y
Include SSP/SMP	Y

To set up employee details

Employee details
Amend employee details
Personal details

Pension ref	1	
NI category	D	
Contracted out	Y	(updates automatically)
Effective date	09/06/95	
Payroll run date	09/06/95	

Run the payroll for week 10 and print out the payslip.

PAYSLIP

		RATE	GROSS PAY	DEDUCTIONS		CUMULATIVES	
Hourly basic:	40.0000	5.0480	201.92	PAYE Tax	31.68	Total gross pay TD	2119.68
Overtime hours:	–	10.0960	–	National Ins.	12.93	Gross for tax TD	2093.64
	–	–	–	Pension	4.04	Tax paid TD	371.98
Bonus:	–	–	–		–	Earnings for NI TD	2113.00
GAYE:	–	–	5.00		–	National Ins. TD	162.62
SAYE:	–	–	6.00		–	Pension TD	4.04
					–		
Sick pay	–	–	–		–	Earnings for NI	201.00
Maternity pay	–	–	–	Rounding b/f	–	Gross for tax	186.88
Holiday pay	–	–	–	Rounding c/f	–	TOTAL GROSS PAY	201.92
						National Ins Number	TR231885H

10	09/06/95	1	CW	250L	2	KEVIN BAKER	Net pay
Week	Date	Dept	Payment	Tax code	Employee ref		£142.27

Week 11

Let us also assume that Kevin has agreed to pay a one-off subscription to the company's *sports and social club*. The weekly amount to deduct from his pay is £19.50 and it is for *one week only*.

Sports and social club subscriptions

Company details
Adjustment types

4 Sports club

This is deducted *after* calculating tax and NICs (so enter – NNN in the adjacent columns).

To set up employee details

Employee details
Amend employee details

Tables selection
Adjustments table 4

The payroll run date for week 11 is 16/06/95. Enter the extra deductions in the payments screen.

PAYSLIP

		RATE	GROSS PAY	DEDUCTIONS		CUMULATIVES	
Hourly basic:	40.0000	5.0480	201.92	PAYE Tax	31.42	Total gross pay TD	2321.60
Overtime hours:	-	10.0960	-	National Ins.	12.93	Gross for tax TD	2280.52
	-	-	-	Pension	4.04	Tax paid TD	403.40
Bonus:	-	-			–	Earnings for NI TD	2314.00
GAYE:	-	-	5.00		–	National Ins. TD	175.55
SAYE:	-	-	6.00		-	Pension TD	8.08
Sports club			19.50		-		
Sick pay	-	-	-		-	Earnings for NI	201.00
Maternity pay	-	-	-	Rounding b/f	-	Gross for tax	186.88
Holiday pay	-	-	-	Rounding c/f	-	TOTAL GROSS PAY	201.92
						National Ins Number	TR231885H

11	16/06/95	1	CW	250L	2	KEVIN BAKER	Net pay
Week	Date	Dept	Payment	Tax code	Employee ref		£123.03

Update the payroll for week 11.

Week 12

Run the payroll of Kevin in week 12 (23rd June). Update the records.

PAYSLIP

		RATE	GROSS PAY	DEDUCTIONS		CUMULATIVES	
Hourly basic:	40.0000	5.0480	201.92	PAYE Tax	31.67	Total gross pay TD	2523.52
Overtime hours:	-	10.0960	-	National Ins.	12.93	Gross for tax TD	2467.40
	-	-	-	Pension	4.04	Tax paid TD	435.07
Bonus:	-	-			–	Earnings for NI TD	2515.00
GAYE:	-	-	5.00		–	National Ins. TD	188.48
SAYE:	-	-	6.00		-	Pension TD	12.12
Sick pay	-	-	-		-	Earnings for NI	201.00
Maternity pay	-	-	-	Rounding b/f	-	Gross for tax	186.88
Holiday pay	-	-	-	Rounding c/f	-	TOTAL GROSS PAY	201.92
						National Ins Number	TR231885H

12	23/06/95	1	CW	250L	2	KEVIN BAKER	Net pay
Week	Date	Dept	Payment	Tax code	Employee ref		£142.28

Week 13

In week 13 (30th June) both Kevin and Jane are to be paid. Run the payroll for both and print out their payslips.

PAYSLIP

		RATE	GROSS PAY	DEDUCTIONS		CUMULATIVES	
Monthly basic:	1.0000	1000.0000	1000.00	PAYE Tax	173.92	Total gross pay TD	3000.00
	–	–	–	National Ins.	80.04	Gross for tax TD	3000.00
	–	–	–	Pension	–	Tax paid TD	521.75
	–	–	–		–	Earnings for NI TD	3000.00
Bonus:	–	–	–		–	National Ins. TD	240.02
	–	–	–		–	Pension TD	–
					–		
Sick pay	–	–	–		–	Earnings for NI	100000
Maternity pay	–	–	–	Rounding b/f	–	Gross for tax	1000.00
Holiday pay	–	–	–	Rounding c/f	–	TOTAL GROSS PAY	1000.00
						National Ins Number	WS278433L

3	30/06/95	2	QM	300L	1	JANE HOWARD	Net pay
Month	Date	Dept	Payment	Tax code	Employee ref		£746.04

		RATE	GROSS PAY	DEDUCTIONS		CUMULATIVES	
Hourly basic:	40.0000	5.0480	201.92	PAYE Tax	31.68	Total gross pay TD	2725.44
Overtime hours:	–	10.0960	-	National Ins.	12.93	Gross for tax TD	2654.28
	–	–	–	Pension	4.04	Tax paid TD	466.75
Bonus:	–	–			–	Earnings for NI TD	2716.00
GAYE:	–	–	5.00		–	National Ins. TD	201.41
SAYE:	–	–	6.00		–	Pension TD	16.16
Sports Club	–	–	15.00		–		
Sick pay	–	–	–		–	Earnings for NI	201.00
Maternity pay	–	–	–	Rounding b/f	–	Gross for tax	186.88
Holiday pay	–	–	–	Rounding c/f	–	TOTAL GROSS PAY	201.92

13	30/06/95	1	CW	250L	2	KEVIN BAKER	Net pay
Week	Date	Dept	Payment	Tax code	Employee ref		£142.27

Changing to monthly pay

Kevin is changing to monthly pay and will be paid by cheque. (Make sure you have closed off week 13 first.) Amend his details to cover the following:

Salary £875 per month
GAYE = £22
SAYE = £26

AT YEAR-END

First of all, we need to get to the year-end!

Run the payroll monthly, paying Kevin his first monthly salary on 28 July 1995 (week 17) and his last on 29th March 1996 (week 52), and Jane as usual.

Remember to update the records after each month.

After processing month 12, exit payroll and return to Sage main menu.

Utilities
Year-end

Print P35, P11 and P14/P60.

The details on the P35 should show the following:

NIC 1	SSP 2	SMP 3	Employee's name 4	Income tax 5
2186.88	0.00	0.00	Jane Howard	2097.75
1277.75	0.00	0.00	Kevin Baker	1697.50
3464.63	0.00	0.00	Grand totals	3785.25

All that remains to do is to run the *year-end routine*. This will clear out all of this year's transactions before moving on to next year. This must not happen until you are sure that you have finished with this year's data.

Emptying transaction files for next year

Utilities
Year end
Payroll
Year-end routines

Clear year TD totals.

This option leaves the employee's standing data intact and should be used if you wish to run through an exercise twice.

WHEN AN EMPLOYEE LEAVES

You must run the payroll for the period up to the date of leaving before removing the employee.

Employee details
Remove an employee

The P11 and P45 will print automatically. Entering a leave date means that the employee is excluded from all future pay runs. The files must *not* be erased because the details are required for the year-end forms.

After running the year-end update, the employee's details will disappear from the system automatically.

WHEN AN EMPLOYEE JOINS

If an employee joins part way through the tax year, you must ensure that you input the details from the P45 correctly.

Employee details
Add a new employee

Screen 3: Banking information

Enter taxable gross pay and tax paid in the box marked P45.

SUPPLEMENTARY INFORMATION

The following information will be of assistance when doing the following assignments.

Setting up employee records

- Payment type:

QM	=	Cheque monthly
CW	=	Cash weekly
GM	=	Giro monthly
GW	=	Giro weekly

- To input week one/month one tax codes (usually 344L) you must enter 344W1 or 344M1 on screen 1.

- Screen 3 – you must always enter total NIC earnings to date if you are starting to computerise payroll part way through the tax year.

To clear data files and start assignments

Return to **C:\SAGE>** prompt in **DOS** and type as follows:

CD COMPANY0	**Return**	
CD PAYDATA	**Return**	(**Note:** There is a space between L and *.)
DEL *.*	**Return**	
Y	**Return**	

This has cleared all standing data from the hard disk. To re-start the exercise put the **Programme disk** in the A drive and follow these instructions.

Switch on and at **C:>** prompt

Type A: then press **return**
Type INSTALL then press **return**

Follow instructions on screen.

In addition, select the **standard default** nominal account structure.

Running software

To run software at **C:>** prompt

Type CD Sage then press **return**
Type Sage then press **return**

Password

See Sage manual or Financial Training Study Planner.

Appendix 1: Using SAGE software

INTRODUCTION

This appendix is designed for use by students studying for this course. It is not designed to be a comprehensive guide and in no way replaces the manuals. SAGE software packages offer the user considerably more functions and features than those described in this Study Pack.

The packages covered in this Study Pack are as follows:

- SAGE Sterling Accountant plus or Financial Controller
- SAGE Sterling Payroll

SAGE Sterling Accountant Plus or Financial Controller

A fully integrated accounting system featuring debtors', creditors' and nominal ledgers.

Invoicing options include trading invoices and freestyle invoices.

The package also offers powerful report generating features.

Note: You can also use these tutorials with SAGE Sterling Accountant but you will not be able to generate sales invoices.

SAGE Sterling Payroll

A complimentary package which can be fully integrated with the above programmes.

The package is a comprehensive payroll package able to cope with all statutory and non-statutory entries and deductions.

Warning

Anyone wishing to use this software in a business environment should not rely on this guide.

In addition, anyone wishing to use SAGE software programs beyond the scope of this course must purchase their own licensed copies of programmes.

SAGE supply a special educational range of software packages. These allow students to use educational versions of SAGE accounting packages on their own PCs at college or at home. Student versions are available to certain educational organisations registered with SAGE.

Please contact SAGE direct on (0191) 201 3000 for further information.

SAGE STERLING ACCOUNTANT PLUS – INTRODUCTION TO COMPUTER SKILLS

Where do you start?

Keyboard

Please note the use of the following keys.

F1	Help key
F2	Displays the calculator
F4	Window for selecting codes etc.
F5	Today's date (for dating transactions)
F6	Repeats the previous field
Shift F6	Increments the previous field
F8	Clears entire field
Esc	Ends the current process. Use this to move back to a higher level.

To choose any option from a menu, use the direction keys to highlight the option and press **Return,** or choose the first letter of the option and press **Return.**

Installation

Switch on and at **C:>** prompt

Type A:	then press **return**
Type INSTALL	then press **return**

Follow instructions on screen.

In addition select the **standard default** nominal account structure.

Running software

To run software at **C:>** prompt

Type CD Sage	then press **return**
Type Sage	then press **return**

Password

See Sage manual or Financial Training Study Planner.

Use the default (pre-set) nominal ledger codes.

Company names

Since the Sage Educational package is not intended for commercial use, you will not be able to alter the company details which appear on invoices and other outputs.

Value added tax (VAT) codings

All transactions entered onto Sage need a VAT code. This is designed to produce an accurate summary for producing a VAT return.

VAT is charged at 17½% on most sales (standard rate). The business then pays this amount to Customs & Excise. The amount due to Customs is reduced by VAT 'suffered' on purchases.

VAT Account

	£		£
VAT on purchases	X	VAT on sales	X
Balance c/f	X		
	–		–
	–		–
		Balance b/f	X
		Due to C&E	–

Sometimes the VAT account will show a debit balance. In this case, Customs owe you a refund.

Although most transactions are standard rated, there are some exceptions:

Zero rated	VAT is charged at 0% on various items including children's' clothes, books, and non-luxury food.
Exempt	These items have no VAT charged on them at all. The category includes rent paid or received, insurance, postal services and bank interest paid or received.

The exact significance of zero rated and exempt supplies is dealt with later on in your studies. For present purposes, all you need to be aware of are the classifications shown above.

SAGE system: VAT codes

Default codes	*VAT rate*	*Used for*
T0	0% (zero)	Sales/purchase of zero-rated items, eg. children's clothes, food.
T1	17½% (standard)	Most other sales or purchases.
T2	Exempt	Rent received or paid. Bank interest received or paid.
T9	N/A	All transactions not affecting VAT returns eg. most journals, opening balances, wages discounts received/allowed cash received from debtors cash paid to creditors.

RECORDING AND ACCOUNTING FOR CASH TRANSACTIONS

To create new customer account

Sales Ledger
Customer Details

To allocate the account reference, use a combination of letters and numbers (eg. A001).

The default VAT code you should use is T1.

Ignore turnover, discount code, analysis code.
Press **Esc** when you have finished with a record.
Select **Post** and press return.
Select **Edit** and press return to amend details.

To print a list of customers

Sales Ledger
Address List

To create new supplier account

Purchase Ledger
Supplier Details

To print a list of suppliers

Purchase Ledger
Address List

To set up nominal codes

Nominal Ledger
Nominal Account Structure
Account Names

Note: The *groups* and *sub-groups* should not be changed; you should only amend the names within these groups or sub-groups (eg. sales, expenses).

Do *not* change the accounts to a different use. Certain accounts (eg. tax control) are posted to automatically by the program and you *cannot* change this. Use *spare* accounts within the correct group or sub-group to add new accounts.

To print a list of nominal ledger codes

Nominal Ledger
Accounts List

To record cash receipts outside the debtors ledger

Either

Nominal Ledger
Bank (or Petty Cash) Transactions
Bank (or Cash) Receipts

or

Nominal Ledger
Journal Entries

This alternative is preferable where the debit entries are *not* all to cash. For entries that do not involve VAT, enter T9 in the column headed Tc (taxcode).

Posting sales invoices

Sales Ledger
Batched Data Entry
Sales Invoice

Note the following entries.

A/C	Press **F4** and select
N/C	Nominal code – press **F4**, then use 4000 Sales
Net amount	Enter amount excluding VAT. The VAT will be automatically calculated if at
Tc	You enter T1 (standard rate)

Press **Esc** and select **Post.** Press Return to post.

Posting purchase invoices

Purchase Ledger
Batched Data Entry
Purchase Invoices

A/C	Press **F4** and select
N/C	Nominal code – press **F4**, then select 5000 Purchases
Tc	T1 (standard rate)

Draft trial balance

Nominal Ledger
Trial Balance

Printing debtors' ledger accounts

Sales Ledger
Transaction History

Printing creditors' ledger accounts

Purchase Ledger
Transaction History

Recording cash receipts

Sales Ledger
Receipts

A/C ref.	Press **F4** and select

Select **manual** payment.

Allocating cash to specific invoices

Select the invoice you wish to pay off (use the direction keys), press enter and select **F** (full).

Allocating cash against oldest invoices

Select **automatic** payment.

To exit, press **Esc** and **P** to post.

To display ledger account

Sales Ledger
Transaction History

Recording cash payments

Purchase Ledger
Payments

To display ledger account

Purchase Ledger
Transaction History

Settlement discounts offered to customers

Sales Ledger
Batched Data Entry
Sales Invoice

The VAT is no longer exactly 17½% of the net sale. You must still use code T1 but now you must manually input the actual VAT charged.

Sales Ledger
Receipts

Enter details (account ref., date, amount, etc.)
Select **manual** payment

Highlight relevant invoice using direction keys, press **Enter** and select **D** (discount).
Enter amount of discount offered and relevant tax code (**T9**, if discount is offered on net amount).

Taking advantage of settlement discounts

Purchase Ledger
Batched Data Entry
Purchase Invoices

As before, use Taxcode T1, but override the automatically calculated VAT amount and input the actual VAT.

Purchase Ledger
Payments

Enter details (account ref., date, amount, etc.)
Select **manual** payment
Highlight relevant invoice using direction keys, press **Enter**
Select **D** (discount). Enter amount of discount offered and relevant tax code (T9).

Note: Discounts obtained from suppliers are netted off against discounts offered to customers, the balance appearing as a separate line, **Discounts**, under sales in the profit and loss account.

Sending out remittance advices

The Sagesoft educational package does not produce the style of Remittance Advice shown in the text.

Transfer cash to petty cash

Nominal Ledger
Journal Entries

Cash/bank payments routine will not deal with transfers to petty cash control.

Petty cash payments

Nominal Ledger
Petty Cash Transactions
Cash Payments

Month-end procedures

For detailed sales/purchase ledger

Sales/Purchase Ledger
Transaction History

Note that any item marked * is unpaid.

For aged analysis of debtors/creditors

Sales/Purchase Ledger
Account Balances (Aged)

Note that any item marked * has a balance in excess of its credit limit.

For management reports

Nominal Ledger
Trial Balance
P&L and Balance Sheet

To create month-end files

Utilities
Month End
Create Month-End Files

This resets the ageing and prepares the files for the next accounting period, and hence should only be done after all the reports have been printed.

(**Note**: If you are using **Financial Controller,** it will also clear out matched transactions.)

Error corrections

To alter an incorrect posting requires the transaction number. This can be identified by selecting **Utilities** from the main menu and then **Audit Trail**.

There are two types of error correction.

(a) Reverse Posting – this cancels the original posting
(b) Correct Posting – this adjusts the original posting

Corrections are carried out as follows.

Utilities
Posting Error Correction
Reverse Posting/Correct Posting

Refunds/Cancelled cheques

Sales (or Purchase) Ledger
Refunds
Cancel Cheque/Refund Invoice
Enter customer account reference and use direction keys to highlight the relevant transaction.

Opening balances on sales/purchase ledger

Sales/Purchase Ledger
Batched Data Entry
Sales/Purchase Invoices

The date used can be the date of the opening balance or, for accurate ageing, the date of the original invoice. The nominal code used should be 'Suspense 9998'. Under 'Details' enter opening balance.

Opening balances should not be split into VAT and Net. Enter the gross balance at 'Net Amount' and use taxcode T9.

Opening balances on trial balance

Nominal ledger
Journal entries
Enter details of opening balances on the relevant accounts, checking that the batch total is zero. Use T9 and under 'Details' enter Opening Balance.

Resetting the transaction files

If you are using **Accountant Plus** you cannot reset the transaction files without losing all standing data. You should therefore not do this until you are certain that you have finished a particular exercise.

Resetting all files

To clear all data:

Utilities
Data file changes
Rebuild data files
Ledger files
No (to existing data)
Yes (to preserve default nominal ledger)

Back-up

When using any software in a business situation, you should make regular daily back-ups.

PRINTING REPORTS

Types of printer

Before printing a report you must select the correct printer option:

Utilities
Defaults
Printer set-up

RECORDING AND ACCOUNTING FOR SALES AND DEBTORS

VAT rates

Utilities
VAT Code Changes – amend as required

Note the pre-set VAT codes are as follows:

T0	zero rated
T1	standard rated
T2	exempt
T4	transactions relating to EC member states
T9	non-VAT rates (outside of scope, eg. settlement discounts)

Setting up product codes

Stock Control
Categories

Allocate categories as required and return to Stock Control menu

Update Stock Details

Enter stock details as required, ensuring correct VAT code is used. The nominal code required is the sales code for the specified category of goods.

Printing out a list of product codes

Stock Control
Stock Details
Select **print** option

Adjusting opening stock

Stock Control
Adjustments In

Raising a sales invoice

Sales Ledger
Invoice Production
Invoicing from Stock

Enter customer account reference at **Sales Ref.** and relevant stock code, amending quantity (set at one unit) if necessary, via the blue sub screen.

Press **Escape** and **Print**

Printing a sales invoice

Sales Ledger
Invoice Production
Print Invoices
Select **print** option

Offering settlement discounts

Sales Ledger
Invoice Production
Invoicing from Stock

As above, but after entering sale items press **F9**. This brings up the **Footing details**. Ignore **carriage values** and move to **settlement values.** Enter the terms (number of days and percentage of discount).

Posting sales invoices

Sales Ledger
Invoice Production
Update Ledgers

The Display Index can be viewed to confirm printing and posting have been done.

Note: The Sage Educational software package has not set up the invoice to show discount deductible although the VAT is calculated correctly.

Printing the aged debtors report

Sales Ledger
Account Balances (Aged)
Select **print** option

Printing out statements of account

Sales Ledger
Statements
Select **print** option

Posting credit notes

Follow procedure for **Raising a Sales Invoice** but select **Credit Note Production** instead of **Invoicing from Stock** from Invoice Production menu.

Remember to use the F9 (Footing) function to discount the VAT.

Bad debts

Sales Ledger
Bad Debt Write-Off

The options available are as follows:

(a) write off an entire account
(b) write off all items below a given amount to be specified (< £100)
(c) write off a single transaction

You will have to identify the **transaction numbers** from the audit trail or you can use the transaction history on screen. Each item within the invoice has a separate transaction number.

Contra entries

Sales Ledger
Contra Entries

Enter relevant sales and purchase accounts and use the direction keys to highlight the transactions to which the contra should apply.

RECORDING AND ACCOUNTING FOR PURCHASES AND CREDITORS

VAT rates

Utilities
VAT Code Changes – amend as required.

Recording purchase invoices

Purchase Ledger
Batched Data Entry
Purchase Invoices – enter details

Use tax code T0 for Trevor Manufacturing, assuming that this company supplies childrens' clothing (zero rated).

Posting credit notes

As above but select **Purchase Credit Notes** instead of **Purchase Invoices** from Batched Data Entry menu.

MAKING PERIOD-END ADJUSTMENTS

Posting cash payments

Nominal Ledger
Bank Transactions
Bank Payments
As Rent is VAT exempt use tax code T2.

Prepayments

Nominal Ledger
Prepayments & Accruals
Prepayments

Either Rent and the Nominal code (7100).
The value is the total rent paid.
The number of months is 12.

Accruals

Nominal Ledger
Prepayment & Accruals
Accruals
Spread £360 over 3 months.

Month-end report

Utilities
Month end
Prepayments & Accruals

Depreciation

Nominal Ledger
Depreciation

The nominal code is that for the accumulated depreciation. There are three types of depreciation policy available:

S = Straight line
R = Reducing balance
W = Write off

Select S.

Month-end

Utilities
Month-end
Depreciation

VAT returns

Nominal Ledger
VAT Return Analysis

Once the report details have been finalised and agreed, you should run a final printout, changing default setting on **Set Reconciliation Flags** to yes.

This will exclude all transactions in this analysis from future VAT analysis.

Once the balance on the VAT return has been agreed to the balance on 2200 (Tax Control), transfer this balance to 2201 via a journal.

Similarly, post opening balances of VAT to 2201.

Appendix 2: Nominal ledger classifications

Sales/turnover/other income

Sales
Sundry income (eg. rent)
Discount received

Cost of sales

Purchases (finished goods, raw materials)

Expenditure

Other expenses (including bad debts)

Fixed assets

Freehold premises
Plant and machinery
Fixtures and fittings
Motor vehicles

Investments

Investments in other companies

Current assets

Stock
Value added tax*
Debtors
Cash at bank and in hand

Current liabilities (creditors falling due within one year)

Creditors
HP creditor
Bank overdraft
Value added tax *
PAYE liability

Long-term liabilities (creditors falling due after one year)

Loans
HP creditor

Capital

Limited company	*Sole trader/partnership*
Share capital	Capital
Share premium	Drawings
Profit and loss account reserve	

***Note**: Value added tax may be a *current asset* or a *current liability*. This depends upon the circumstances of the individual entity.

Assignments

ASSIGNMENT 1: GEORGE JONES, SCRAPMERCHANTS

Element 1 Input information from source documents into a computer system

- All vital fields are completed
- Incomplete or unauthorised source documents are referred for clarification
- All errors in inputting and coding are identified and corrected
- Correct part of the computer system is used for inputting

  New unique reference codes are generated as necessary
- Inputting is completed to agreed deadline

  Organisational procedures for filing source documents are followed
- Risks to the information technology environment are minimised at all times

Range

Information

- words
- numbers
- information to be coded

Source documents

- complete
- incomplete

Computer systems

- databases

  spreadsheets

Types of inputting

- addition of new info

  modification of existing info

  deletion/cancellation

Databases

stock control
- customers
- sales ledgers
- purchase ledgers

employees

cash logs

Unique reference numbers

- stock codes
- customer references
- invoice numbers
- employee numbers

FACTFILE

Business name	George Jones Scrapmerchants
Address	134 High Street Lees Oldham OL4 6ER
Telephone	0161 626 7788
Fax	0161 626 4922
VAT Reg. No.	411 2344 98
Personnel	George Jones – the boss Betty Foster – does all the paperwork
Business	Buying and selling all types of scrap metal
Type of business entity	Sole trader
Number of accounts	20 each for customers and suppliers

Business profile

Business has always been good.

George has dealt with most of the customers for years. They either collect the scrap from the yard or George delivers it in the business's van.

He does not expect immediate payment from his long standing customers, so they send cheques or postal orders by post.

Occasionally casual customers turn up at the yard to buy odd bits of scrap. They must pay cash.

The ledgers have recently been transferred to a computerised system.

Terms of trade

The business has recently registered for VAT. All customers have a credit limit of £500.

A 2% discount is offered on all invoices which are paid within 30 days of the invoice date.

None of the business's suppliers offers settlement discounts.

YOUR ASSIGNMENT

Today is 30 April 19**.

You are required to set up the standing data within the computerised ledger system.

You are then required to enter the transactions for April from the cash book into the computerised ledger system.

Print out the **nominal ledger listing** (trial balance) (individual accounts are not required).

Print out individual **ledger accounts** in the debtors' and creditors' ledgers.

File any **audit trails** at the back of your work.

STANDING DATA

Customers

Code	*Name*	*Address*	*Contact*	*VAT No.*
1	J F Lawrence	22 Dougal Street Chadderton Oldham OL9 9TH Tel: 0161 626 5536	John Lawrence	111 2222 33
2	Acme Scrap	Horseshoe Lane Overton Preston PR5 3RF Tel: 0161 335 7686	Sid Fredericks	222 3333 44
3	Alfred Stocker	Sam Road Diggle Oldham OL15 4PL Tel: 0161 667 2349	Alfred Stocker	333 4444 55
4	Foster Brothers	409 Edgeware Street Newton Heath Manchester M3 4ED Tel: 0161 236 7766	Edward Foster	444 5555 66

5	Palatine Supplies	404 Palatine Road Withington Manchester M20 Tel: 0161 338 8769	George Fox	555 1666 77
6	Sid Pearl	Scrapmerchants 48 Canal Walk Newton Heath Manchester M3 7BJ Tel: 0161 366 9880	Sid Pearl	666 7777 88
7	Terrence James & Co Ltd	35 Fleet Road Beswick Manchester M28 6EW Tel: 0161 334 4566	Terrence James	777 8888 99
8	Proctor & Proctor	366 New Earth Street Leeds Oldham OL4 8BE Tel: 0161 366 8678	Fred Proctor	888 9999 00

Suppliers

Code	*Name*	*Address*	*Contact*	*VAT No.*
1	Graham Metals	167 Fortune Street Clayton Manchester M16 4MC Tel: 0161 488 7677	John Graham	121 3333 99
2	C R Carson	219 Merry Street Chadderton Oldham OL9 5WF Tel: 0161 776 4533	Charlie Carson	232 4444 99
3	Derek Taylor & Co	359 Diggle Road Uppermill Oldham OL14 5GJ Tel: 0161 244 5787	Derek Taylor	343 5555 99

4	S R Grant	Old Works Priest Lane Middleton M36 9US Tel: 0161 377 4566	Steve Grant	454 6666 99
5	Davies and Hughes	Allen Street St Marys Oldham OL1 4EL Tel: 0161 337 8799	Terry Davies	565 7777 99
6	Yates' Yard	Whitely Lane Prestwich Manchester M14 4MF Tel: 0161 377 6733	Ted Boulton	676 8888 99

Opening balances

Code	*Account*	*Invoice*	*Net*	*VAT*	*Gross*
			£	£	£
1	JF Lawrence	1032	34.68	5.94	40.62
2	Acme Scrap	1027	27.44	4.70	32.14
3	Alfred Stocker	1040	36.48	6.25	42.73
4	Foster Brothers	1023	18.90	3.24	22.14
5	Palatine Supplies	1038	267.90	45.94	313.84
6	Sid Pearl Scrapmerchants	1025	344.98	59.16	404.14
		1039	27.99	4.80	32.79
7	Terrence James & Co Ltd	1024	189.30	32.46	221.76
		1041	45.77	7.84	53.61
8	Proctor & Proctor	1026	18.90	3.24	22.14
		1028	122.48	21.00	143.48
	Total				1,329.39
1	Graham Metals	2399	112.45	19.67	132.12
2	C R Carson	2396	54.39	9.51	63.90
		2400	130.89	22.90	153.79
3	Derek Taylor & Co	2397	99.09	17.34	116.43
4	S R Grant	2401	178.67	31.26	209.93
5	Davies and Hughes	2403	23.46	4.10	27.56
6	Yates' Yard	2398	28.90	5.05	33.95
		2402	174.98	30.62	205.60
	Totals				943.28

Nominal codes and opening balances

		Dr £	Cr £
4000	Sales		14,689.34
5000	Purchases	8,813.40	
4009	Discounts allowed	212.60	
7003	Staff salaries	2,435.78	
7200	Electricity	443.66	
7502	Telephone	245.89	
7504	Office stationery	123.90	
6900	Miscellaneous expenses	87.40	
7900	Bank interest	122.45	
0020	Plant and machinery	5,219.95	
1100	Debtors	1,329.39	
2200	Tax control		514.15
1200	Current account		2,344.68
1230	Petty cash	70.00	
2100	Creditors		943.28
3000	Ordinary shares		2,000.00
3200	Profit & loss account		1,068.64
1001	Stock	2,455.67	
		21,560.09	21,560.09

CASH BOOK RECEIPTS

Date	Narrative	Invoices paid	Folio	Account code	Bank £	VAT £	Discount £
3/4	Foster Brothers	1023	DL	4	22.14		
7/4	Cash sale		NL	1	73.48	10.94	
10/4	George Fox	1038	DL		308.48		5.36
14/4	JF Lawrence	1032	DL	1	39.93		0.69
17/4	Terrence James & Co	1024	DL	7	221.76		
21/4	Cash sale		NL	1	44.66	6.65	
23/4	Sid Pearl	1025, 1039	DL	6	436.38		0.55
24/4	Acme Scrap	1027	DL	2	32.14		
28/4	Cash sale		NL	1	89.33	13.30	
29/4	Capital: New shares issued		NL		5,000.00		
	Totals				6268.30	30.89	6.60

CASH BOOK PAYMENTS

Date	Narrative	Cheque no.	Invoices paid	Folio	Account code	Cash £	Bank £	VAT £	Discount £	Stationery £
12/4	Stationery	233		NL						50
15/4	Graham Metals	234	2399	CL	1		132.12			
15/4	CR Carson	235	2396	CL	2		63.90			
15/4	Derek Taylor	236	2397	CL	3		116.43			
15/4	Yates' Yard	237	2398	CL	6		33.95			
29/4	Wages – Betty	238		NL	54		395.44			
29/4	Fixed assets	239		NL	134		1,566.34	233.28		
29/4	English Telecomm	SO		NL	62		137.66	20.50		
29/4	Petty cash	–		NL	166	38.75				
30/4	Bank interest/charges	–		NL	115		23.45			
	Totals					38.75	2,469.29	253.78		50

PETTY CASH BOOK

Receipts £	Date	Details	Voucher	Total payment £	Analysis					
					VAT	Stationery	Postage	Travel	Sundries	Other
70.00	1/4	b/f								
	3/4	Stamps	67	6.55			6.55			
	14/4	Taxi	68	2.50				2.50		
	16/4	Rail fare	69	11.45				11.45		
	20/4	Stamps	70	3.45			3.45			
	22/4	Coffee etc.	71	8.09	1.20				6.89	
	24/4	Stationery	72	4.04	0.60	3.44				
	28/4	Cleaning goods	73	2.67					2.67	
38.75	29/4									
				38.75	1.80	3.44	10.00	13.95	9.56	
	30/4	c/f		70.00						
108.75				108.75						

ASSIGNMENT 2: PAPERBOX EXPRESS LTD

Element 3 Generate and print standard reports on a computer system

- Required range and report correctly specified
- Printed information is correct and complete
- Hard copy is clean, clearly printed and aligned correctly
- Efforts are made to minimise the wastage of paper
- Printer area is kept clean and tidy
- Work is produced to agreed deadline
- Documents are correctly collated and distributed as directed
- Risks to the information technology environment are minimised at all time

Range

Generation

- specification of start and finish
- selection of required report

Standard reports

bar charts
pie charts
histograms
- standard database reports

Computer systems

- databases

spreadsheets

Standard database reports

- invoices

payments
pay runs
- statements of account

infringement reports
flexitime reports

FACTFILE

Business name	Paperbox Express Ltd

Address	Braebank Mill Inverkip Road Greenock PA16 8FT	
Telephone	01475 33446	
Fax	01475 36778	
VAT Reg. No.	220 5564 12	
Number of accounts required	20 each (debtors, creditors and products)	
Personnel	Managing director Sales director Financial director Financial controller Ledger assistant	Lothar Meyer Tony Bernadotti Adrian Eastwood Angela Rumbold You
Business	Wholesale of computer stationery supplies	

Business profile

Paperbox Ltd was started in 1975 by Lothar Meyer and Tony Bernadotti. Originally the business was a partnership, but in 1985 the partners formed a limited company.

That company now sells a wide variety of stationery products by mail order and to stationery retailers. A sales team covers the whole country, visiting retailers. The company produces a catalogue twice a year.

Following the success of Paperbox Ltd the directors set up Paperbox Express Ltd. This company offers rapid despatch on a small range of computer accessories.

The company has been financed mostly by a loan from the parent company. It has no fixed assets.

Terms of trade

Sales to retailers are on credit terms. Normal terms are a 2% discount for invoices paid within 14 days of the invoice date. All invoices are payable within 30 days. All customers have a credit limit of £1,000.

The company is registered for VAT. VAT is charged on all supplies made by the company at standard rate.

The company buys goods from a limited number of suppliers.

Sales and despatch procedures

Sales orders are taken by the telesales team. A record of all sales orders is kept centrally. Goods are then despatched from one of four sites around the country.

Goods despatched are accompanied by a despatch note. Sales invoices are prepared from a listing of despatch notes. All sales invoices are issued and recorded centrally.

Purchasing procedures

Invoices are approved, coded and batched prior to input. The source document for inputting is the *batch summary*.

YOUR ASSIGNMENT

The company has only been trading for two days.

1 You have just received the first details of despatches from around the country. You are required to generate a **sales invoice** for each despatch. Print out **audit trails** for filing.

   Two copies of each invoice should be produced. (You may use multi-copy stationery if supplies are available.)

2 You have also received a purchase invoice **batch summary**. You are required to input the details shown on the summary. Print out **audit trails** for filing.

3 Print out the **trial balance** at the end of processing. Individual ledger accounts (debtors', creditors' and nominal) are **not** required.

4 Print out an **aged debtors' listing** and a **creditors' listing**.

5 Prepare **statements of account** to send to customers.

Paperbox Express Ltd
Product Listing

Code	*Product*	*Size/colour*	*Price (excl. VAT)* £
1	Datasaver envelope	330 × 254mm	104.02
2	(100)	406 × 304mm	137.64
3	Diskbox	5 1/4"	12.95
4		3 1/2"	9.95
5	Expanding diskbox	3 1/2"	10.95
6	Multibox	5 1/4"	21.95
7		3 1/2"	18.95
8	Microfiche ring binder	325 × 272mm	14.60
9	Labels (10,000 box)	89 × 37mm	48.50
10		102 × 37mm	51.00
11		89 × 49mm	71.20
12		102 × 49mm	71.20
13		127 × 49mm	83.70
14	Printout paper (2,000)	279 × 370mm	31.57
15	Multicopy 2-part (1,000)	295 × 235mm	54.22
16	Multicopy 3-part (700)	295 × 235mm	56.86
17	Re-cyclone (1,000)	279 × 370mm	25.98
18	Printout binder	Black	52.60
19	(universal) (10)	Blue	52.60
20		Red	52.60

Paperbox Express Ltd
Nominal code listing (extract)

4000	Sales A (Computer supplies)
5000	Purchases (Computer supplies)
4009	Discounts allowed
1100	Debtors
2200	Tax control account
2100	Creditors control
3000	Share capital
2300	Loan creditors (Inter-company)
1001	Stock

Before recording the first trading transactions the company has share capital of £2.00, stock of £4,765.96, VAT recoverable of £834.04 and an inter-company loan of £5,598.00.

DESPATCH RECORD

No.	*Customer*	*VAT Reg.*	*Product No.*	*Quantity*
1	Abraham and Matthews Ltd 152 High Street Romford Essex RM1 1JU	111 2222 33 GB	5 6 12	24 10 3
2	Qwerty Office Supplies 192 High Street Barnet Herts EN6 4ES	444 5555 66 GB	14 15 18	1 1 1
3	Ronald Earl Group Limited 245 Holliday Street Birmingham B1 5VT	777 8888 99 GB	1 4	2 3
4	Giftbox Ltd 76 Queensway Redhill Surrey RH1 3WE	010 1212 33 GB	13 18	2 2
5	Denton Stationery Suppliers 87 Crown Street Guide Bridge Manchester M23 4EF	222 3333 44 GB	11 13 18 19	1 3 3 1

PURCHASE INVOICE BATCH SUMMARY

Inv. No.	*Supplier*	*Supplier ref.*	*NL code*	*Net* £	*VAT* £	*Gross* £
1	First Class Supplies	1	5000	344.78	60.34	405.12
2	Computerise Ltd	3	5000	123.89	21.68	145.57
3	Plastics Unlimited	5	5000	445.66	77.99	523.65
4	Davidson Stationers Ltd	2	5000	234.55	41.05	275.60
5	Paper Products Ltd	4	5000	2,988.89	523.06	3,511.95
				4,137.77	724.12	4,861.89

SUPPLIER DETAILS

		VAT No.	*Credit limit*
1	First Class Supplies 56 The Cross Worcester WR1 2PQ	333 4545 66 GB	3,000
2	Davidson Stationers Ltd 23 St Andrews Street Cambridge CB2 3AH	555 6767 88 GB	3,000
3	Computerise Ltd 288 West Regent Street Coventry CV1 5DF	666 7878 99 GB	3,000
4	Paper Products Ltd 199 Spon Street Glasgow G2 2RQ	888 9090 11 GB	3,000
5	Plastics Unlimited 18 Belvoir Way Colchester CO1 2FG	999 0101 22 GB	3,000

ASSIGNMENT 3: JP HARTNELL LTD

Element 1 Input information from source documents into a computer system

- All vital fields are completed
- Incomplete or unauthorised source documents are referred for clarification
- All errors in inputting and coding are identified and corrected
- Correct part of the computer system is used for inputting
- New unique reference codes are generated as necessary
- Inputting is completed to agreed deadline
- Organisational procedures for filing source documents are followed
- Risks to the information technology environment are minimised at all time

Range

Information

- words
- numbers
- information to be coded

Source documents

- complete
- incomplete

Computer systems

- databases
- spreadsheets

Types of inputting

- addition of new info
- modification of existing info
- deletion/cancellation

Databases

- stock control
- customers
- sales ledgers
- purchase ledgers
- employees
- cash logs

Unique reference numbers

- stock codes
- customer references
- invoice numbers
- employee numbers

Element 3 Generate and print standard reports on a computer system

- Required range and report correctly specified
- Printed information is correct and complete
- Hard copy is clean, clearly printed and aligned correctly
- Efforts are made to minimise the wastage of paper
- Printer area is kept clean and tidy
- Work is produced to agreed deadline
- Documents are correctly collated and distributed as directed
- Risks to the information technology environment are minimised at all time

Range

Generation

- specification of start and finish
- selection of required report

Standard reports

- bar charts
- pie charts
- histograms
- standard database reports

Computer systems

- databases
- spreadsheets

Standard database reports

- invoices
- payments
- pay runs
- statements of account infringement reports
- flexitime reports

FACTFILE

Business name	JP Hartnell Ltd
Address	Thelwell Works Thelwell Road Solihull B90 0AY
Location	Four manufacturing sites in Warrington, Consett, Hastings and Solihull Head office in Milton Keynes
Business	Manufacture and distribution of doors
Bank details	Glynns & Williams Bank plc 5 Main Road Solihull
Sort code	99–88–77

Business profile

Each of the four manufacturing sites is responsible for its own purchases of goods and services from suppliers (including heat, light and power).

Each site also pays its own wages and salaries.

Solihull site

The Solihull site manufactures the company's full range of doors then distributes them with its fleet of lorries.

Personnel

Operations manager	Neil McCann
Finance manager	Paul Snow
Accounts assistant	You

Your responsibilities include preparing the payroll.

Payroll processing

Payroll is prepared weekly for production staff and monthly for other staff. All staff are currently paid by cheque.

Production staff are paid based on hours worked recorded on clock cards.

Certain of the sales staff are paid a commission as well as a basic salary. This is based on sales figures from the previous month.

YOUR ASSIGNMENT

You are required to prepare the wages of one production worker and one of the salesmen.

Part one

Here is the standing data for the two employees.

Employee 1

Surname	Partridge
First name	Trevor
Title	Mr
NI number	HJ 45 23 12 J
Tax code	352L
Tax basis	Normal cumulative
Department code	1
Birth date	4–2–55
Join date	3–5–75
Director	No
Payment method	Cheque
Pay frequency	Weekly
Rate of pay	£4.67 per hour
Hours worked	38 per week
NI letter	A
Address	56 Pleasant Avenue Solihull B90 4DF
Marital status	Single

Employee 2

Surname	Kershaw
First name	Andrew
Title	Mr
NI number	LK 34 87 55 K
Tax code	150T
Tax basis	Normal cumulative
Department code	2
Birth date	6–3–65
Join date	7–5–89
Director	No
Payment method	Cheque
Pay frequency	Monthly
Rate indicator	A
Rate of pay	£9,000 plus commission
NI letter	A
Address	56 Walnut Way Ashton Solihull B90 8YH
Marital status	Single

Part two

Run the first week and the first month's payroll after making the following wages and salary adjustments.

Trevor Partridge has worked his basic week plus 5 hours overtime at time and a half.

Andrew Kershaw has earned commission of £289.99.

Part three

Print out the following reports:

- payslips;
- cheques (or cheque listing);
- payroll summary;
- PAYE remittance report.

Answers to questions

SESSION 1

Answer

Receipts

Proceeds from sale of fixed assets
VAT refunds
Capital received from owners of the business
Long-term loans received

Payments

Wages and salaries
VAT payments
PAYE payments
Purchases of fixed assets
Capital repaid
Long-term loans repaid

(*This is not a comprehensive list.*)

SESSION 2

Answer 1

		Code	£
Dr	Cash at bank	1200	7,500
	Stock	1001	2,500
Cr	Share capital	3000	10,000

Answer 2

		Code	£
Dr	Debtors control account	1100	663.66
Cr	Sales type A	4000	564.82
	Tax control	2200	98.84

Answer 3

This is the total amount which is owed by the customer.

Answer 4

This is the true value of the sales made by the business. The VAT charged is not part of the business's sales. The business is acting as a tax collector on behalf of HM Customs and Excise.

Answer 5

Revenue
Asset
Liability

Answer 6

		Code	£
Dr	Materials purchases	5000	319.76
	Tax control	2200	55.97
Cr	Creditors control	2100	375.73

Answer 7

There is no permanent printed record of the entries (ie. a day book).

This can be overcome by printing out an *audit trail* whenever new data is introduced into the system. You should do this as a matter of course when completing a devolved assessment.

Answer 8

Greensleeves Ltd
Trial balance

		Dr £	*Cr* £
1001	Stock	2,500.00	
1100	Debtors control	563.66	
1200	Bank	7,500.00	
2100	Creditors control		375.73
2200	VAT control		42.87
3000	Ordinary shares		10,000.00
4000	Sales type A		564.82
5000	Material purchases	319.76	
		10,983.42	10,983.42

The two columns must be equal.

Answer 9

The information which has been posted to the account in the nominal ledger and the individual accounts in the debtors' or creditors' ledger came from exactly the same source. The totals were posted to the nominal ledger accounts and the detail to the *debtors'* and *creditors' ledger accounts*.

Answer 10

		Code	£
Dr	Bank current account	1200	663.67
Cr	Debtors control account	1100	663.67

Answer 11

Reconciling the balance per the nominal ledger account for cash at bank to the balance per the cash book. (This is in addition to the bank reconciliation between cash book and bank statement.)

Answer 12

From the *remittance* advices which they send with their payments.

Answer 13

		Code	£
Dr	Bank current account	1200	446.43
	Discounts allowed	4009	7.74
Cr	Debtors control account	1100	454.17

Answer 14

The customer would pay the total as invoiced. The customer would not be expected to pay the extra VAT. This practice has been agreed by HM Customs & Excise as a practical solution to an otherwise difficult problem.

Answer 15

	Cash £	*Discount* £
Farmer Manufacturing Ltd	194.30	2.51

Answer 16

		Code	£
Dr	Creditors control	2100	196.81
Cr	Cash at bank	1200	194.30
	Discounts taken	5009	2.51

Answer 17

		Code	£
Dr	Bank current account	1200	416.24
Cr	Sales	4000	354.25
	Tax control	2200	61.99

Answer 18

The VAT charge is accounted at this stage because this is the first point at which the sale is recorded. Cash from debtors is outside of the scope of VAT because the VAT charge was accounted for when the sale was first recorded.

Answer 19

		Code	£
Dr	Materials purchases	5000	98.56
	Miscellaneous expenses	6900	34.44
	Tax control	2200	17.24
Cr	Bank current account	1200	150.24

Answer 20

		Code	£
Dr	Petty cash	1230	150.00
Cr	Bank current account	1200	150.00

Answer 21

The cash book (for the main bank account).

Answer 22

		Code	£
Dr	Materials purchases	5000	22.34
	Miscellaneous expenses	6900	11.38
	VAT	2200	4.22
Cr	Petty cash	1230	37.94

SESSION 4

Answer 1

Receipts from debtors
Payments to creditors
Capital receipts from the owners of the business
Wages and salaries

(*This is not a comprehensive list*.)

Answer 2

		Code	£
Dr	Debtors	1100	76.99
Cr	Sales 1 – men's	4000	22.50
	Sales 2 – women's	4001	26.00
	Sales 3 – children's	4002	20.00
	VAT	2200	8.49

Answer 3

		Code	£
Dr	Debtors	1100	16.40
Cr	Sales A – men's	4000	7.50
	Sales B – women's	4001	6.50
	Tax control	2200	2.40

Answer 4

		Code	£
Dr	Sales B – women's	4001	26.00
	Tax control	2200	4.46
Cr	Debtors control account	1100	30.46

Answer 5

		Code	£
Dr	Bad debt write-off	8100	118.70
Cr	Debtors control account	1100	118.70

Answer 6

		£
Dr	Creditors	234.55
Cr	Debtors	234.55

Answer 7

		Code	£
Dr	Contras (suspense)	9998	234.55
Cr	Debtors control account	1100	234.55
Dr	Creditors control account	2100	234.55
Cr	Contras (suspense)	9998	234.55

Note how the *net effect* (ie. after cancelling out the two contra entries) is the same as the first double-entry.

SESSION 5

Answer 1

Standard rate
Zero-rate
Exempt
Outside of scope

Answer 2

		Code	£
Dr	Purchases A – Men's	5001	152.33
	Purchases B – Women's	5002	227.99
	Purchases C – Children's	5003	111.92
	Tax control account	2200	66.56
Cr	Creditors control account	2100	558.80

Answer 3

Credit notes are posted to the accounts in both the debtors' and creditors' ledgers. The nominal ledger entry for each credit note is a contras account.

The entries in the contras account net out to give a nil balance.

Answer 4

Outside the scope of VAT, but the amount of VAT is £0.00.

SESSION 6

Answer 1

		Code	£
Dr	Prepayment	1103	1,380
Cr	Rent	7100	1,380

Answer 2

		Code	£
Dr	Rent (1,380 ÷ 12)	7100	115
Cr	Prepayments	1103	115

Answer 3

4,000 × 25% = £1,000 depreciation per annum

Answer 4

1,000 ÷ 12 = 83.33

	Code	£
Dr O/E depreciation (expense)	8004	83.33
Cr O/E depreciation (provision)	0031	83.33

SESSION 7

Answer 1

Income tax deducted
plus
NI contributions deducted
less
Recoverable amounts of SSP and SMP

Answer 2

Basic pay
Overtime pay
Holiday pay
Bonus
Commission
Statutory sick pay
Statutory maternity pay

(*This is not an all inclusive list.*)

Answer 3

Superannuation payments (pension contributions)
Attachment of earnings payments
Payments under the Save As You Earn (SAYE) scheme
Payments under the Give As You Earn (GAYE) scheme (payroll giving)
Other payments, eg. subscriptions to sports and social clubs

Answer 4

Superannuation payments, but *only* if the payments are to an occupational pension scheme *approved* by the Inland Revenue

Payments under the Save As You Earn (SAYE) scheme

Payments under the Give As You Earn (GAYE) scheme

Solutions to assignments

ASSIGNMENT 1: GEORGE JONES, SCRAPMERCHANTS

Note: When inputting the opening debtors' and creditors' balances, the full value of invoices must be allocated to the nominal code for suspense, not sales, as these invoices have already been accounted for in an earlier period.

Double-entry

(This is shown for the sake of completeness. Remember that receipts from creditors/debtors are posted through the purchase/sales ledgers and other items are posted through the nominal ledger.)

		Code	£	£
Dr	Bank current account	1200	6,268.30	
	Discounts allowed	4009	6.60	
Cr	Debtors (1,060.83 + 6.60)	1100		1,067.43
	Sales	4000		176.58
	Tax control	2200		30.89
	Ordinary shares	3000		5,000.00

To record cash receipts

		Code	£	£
Dr	Office stationery	7504	50.00	
	Creditors	2100	346.40	
	Wages	7003	395.44	
	Telephone	7502	117.16	
	Fixed assets	0020	1,333.06	
	Petty cash	1230	38.75	
	Bank interest/charges	7900	23.45	
	Tax control	2200	253.78	
Cr	Bank current account	1200		2,558.04

To record cash payments

Dr	Tax control	2200	1.80	
	Stationery	7504	3.44	
	Postage (sundry)	6900	10.00	
	Travel (sundry)	6900	13.95	
	Miscellaneous	6900	9.56	
Cr	Petty cash	1230		38.75

To record petty cash payments

George Jones Scrapmerchants Ltd
Trial Balance

		£	£
0020	Plant and machinery	6,553.01	
1001	Stock	2,455.67	
1100	Debtors control	261.96	
1200	Bank current account	1,365.58	
1230	Petty cash	70.00	
2100	Creditors		596.88
2200	Tax control		289.46
3000	Ordinary shares		7,000.00
3200	P&L account		1,068.64
4000	Sales		14,865.92
4009	Discounts allowed	219.20	
5000	Purchases	8,813.40	
6900	Miscellaneous expenses	120.91	
7003	Staff salaries	2,831.22	
7200	Electricity	443.66	
7502	Telephone	363.05	
7504	Office stationery	177.34	
7900	Bank interest	145.90	
		23,820.90	23,820.90

George Jones Scrapmerchants Ltd
Sales Ledger Reports – Transaction History

Date: *
Page: *

Account 1: JF Lawrence

No.	Tp	Date	Ref	N/C	Details	Value	Debit	Credit	V	B
*	SI	*	1032	9998	Opening balance	40.62	40.62			
*	SR	*	–	1200	Sales receipt	40.62		40.62		B

Amount outstanding:	0
Amount paid this period:	40.62
Credit limit:	500.00
Turnover year to date:	40.62

Account 2: ACME Scrap

No.	Tp	Date	Ref	N/C	Details	Value	Debit	Credit	V	B
*	SI	*	1027	9998	Opening balance	32.14	32.14			
*	SR	*	–	1200	Sales receipt	32.14		32.14		B

Amount outstanding:	0
Amount paid this period:	–
Credit limit:	500.00
Turnover year to date:	32.14

Account 3: Alfred Stocker

No.	Tp	Date	Ref	N/C	Details	Value	Debit	Credit	V	B
*	SI	*	1040	9998	Opening balance	42.73	42.73			

Amount outstanding:	42.73
Amount paid this period:	0
Credit limit:	500.00
Turnover year to date:	42.73

Account 4: Foster Brothers

No.	Tp	Date	Ref	N/C	Details	Value	Debit	Credit	V	B
*	SI	*	1023	9998	Opening balance	22.14	22.14			
*	SR	*	–	1200	Sales receipt	22.14		22.14	V	

Amount outstanding:	0
Amount paid this period:	22.14
Credit limit:	500.00
Turnover year to date:	22.14

Account 5: Palatine Supplies

No.	Tp	Date	Ref	N/C	Details	Value	Debit	Credit	V	B
*	SI	*	1038	9998	Opening balance	313.84	313.84			
*	SR	*	–	1200	Sales receipt	313.84		313.84		B

Amount outstanding: 0
Amount paid this period: 313.84
Credit limit: 500.00
Turnover year to date: 313.84

Account 6: Sid Pearl Scrapmerchants

No.	Tp	Date	Ref	N/C	Details	Value	Debit	Credit	V	B
*	SI	*	1025	9998	Opening balance	404.14*	404.14			
*	SR	*	1039	9998	Sales receipt	32.79*	32.79			

Amount outstanding: 436.93
Amount paid this period: 0
Credit limit: 500.00
Turnover year to date: 436.93

Account 7: Terrence James & Co Ltd

No.	Tp	Date	Ref	N/C	Details	Value	Debit	Credit	V	B
*	SI	*	1024	9998	Opening balance	221.76	221.76			
*	SI	*	1041	9998	Opening balance	53.61*	53.61			
*	SR	*		1200	Sales receipts	221.76		221.76		B

Amount outstanding: 53.61
Amount paid this period: 221.76
Credit limit: 500.00
Turnover year to date: 275.37

Account 8: Proctor & Proctor

No.	Tp	Date	Ref	N/C	Details	Value	Debit	Credit	V	B
*	SI	*	1026	9998	Opening balance	22.14*				
*	SI	*	1028	9998	Opening balance	143.48*				

Amount outstanding: 165.62
Amount paid this period: 0
Credit limit: 500.00
Turnover year to date: 165.62

Creditors Ledger – George Jones Scrapmerchants Ltd
Purchase Ledger Reports – Transaction History

Account 1: Graham Metals

No.	Tp	Date	Ref	N/C	Details	Value	Debit	Credit	V	B
*	PI	*	2399	9998	Opening balance	132.12		132.12	V	
*	PP	*	234	1200	Purchase payment	132.12	132.12			B

Amount outstanding:	0
Amount paid this period:	132.12
Credit limit:	0.00
Turnover year to date:	132.12

Account 2: CR Carson

No.	Tp	Date	Ref	N/C	Details	Value	Debit	Credit	V	B
*	PI	*	2396	9998	Opening balance	63.90		63.90	V	
*	PP	*	2400	9998	Opening balance	153.79*		153.79	V	
*	PP	*	235	1200	Purchase payment	63.90	63.90			B

Amount outstanding:	153.79
Amount paid this period:	63.90
Credit limit:	0.00
Turnover year to date:	217.69

Account 3: Dereck Taylor & Co

No.	Tp	Date	Ref	N/C	Details	Value	Debit	Credit	V	B
*	PI	*	2397	9998	Opening balance	116.43		116.43	V	
*	PP	*	236	1200	Sales receipt	116.43	116.43			B

Amount outstanding:	0
Amount paid this period:	116.43
Credit limit:	0.00
Turnover year to date:	116.43

Account 4: SR Grant

No.	Tp	Date	Ref	N/C	Details	Value	Debit	Credit	V	B
*	PI	*	2401	9998	Opening balance	209.93*		209.93*	V	

Amount outstanding:	209.93
Amount paid this period:	0.00
Credit limit:	0.00
Turnover year to date:	209.93

Account 5: Davies and Hughes

No.	Tp	Date	Ref	N/C	Details	Value	Debit	Credit	V	B
*	PI	*	2403	9998	Opening balance	27.56*		27.56	V	

Amount outstanding:	27.56
Amount paid this period:	0.00
Credit limit:	0.00
Turnover year to date:	27.56

Account 6: Yates Yard

No.	Tp	Date	Ref	N/C	Details	Value	Debit	Credit	V	B
*	PI	*	2398	9998	Opening balance	33.95		33.95	V	
*	PI	*	2402	9998	Opening balance	205.60*		205.60	V	
*	PP	*	234	1200	Purchase payment	33.95	33.95			B

Amount outstanding:	205.60
Amount paid this period:	33.95
Credit limit:	0.00
Turnover year to date:	239.55

ASSIGNMENT 2: PAPERBOX EXPRESS LTD

Trial balance

		£	£
4000	Sales 1 – Computer supplies		1,877.48
5000	Purchases 1 – Computer supplies	4,137.77	
4009	Discounts given		
1100	Debtors	2,199.47	
2200	Tax control	1,236.17	
2100	Creditors		4,861.89
3000	Share capital		2.00
2300	Loan creditors		5,598.00
1001	Stock	4,765.96	
		12,339.37	12,339.37

Note that discounts given are not accounted for until the cash is received from the customer.

Paperbox Express Ltd
Braebank Mill
Inverkip Road
Greenock
PA16 8FT

Tel: 01475 33446
Fax: 01475 36778

VAT No: 220 5564 12

Abraham and Matthews Ltd
152 High Street
Romford
Essex
RM1 1JU

INVOICE

INVOICE NO.	1
DATE/TAX POINT	*
ACCOUNT REF.	001

QUANTITY	DETAILS	DISC	NET PRICE	VAT
24	Expanding diskbox	0.00	262.80	45.07
10	Multibox 5 1/4	0.00	219.50	37.64
3	Labels 102 × 49	0.00	213.60	36.63
... AS INVOICED ...			*NET*	695.90
			VAT	119.34
			TOTAL	815.24

Paperbox Express Ltd
Braebank Mill
Inverkip Road
Greenock
PA16 8FT

Tel: 01475 33446
Fax: 01475 36778

VAT No: 220 5564 12

Qwerty Office Supplies
192 High Street
Barnet
Herts
EN6 4ES

INVOICE

INVOICE NO.	2
DATE/TAX POINT	*
ACCOUNT REF.	002

QUANTITY	DETAILS	DISC	NET PRICE	VAT
1	Printout 2000	0.00	31.57	5.41
1	Multicopy 2-part	0.00	54.22	9.30
1	Printer binder	0.00	52.60	9.02
... AS INVOICED ...			*NET*	138.39
			VAT	23.73
			TOTAL	162.12

Paperbox Express Ltd
Braebank Mill
Inverkip Road
Greenock
PA16 8FT

Tel: 01475 33446
Fax: 01475 36778

VAT No: 220 5564 12

Ronald Earl Group Ltd
245 Holliday Street
Birmingham
B1 5VT

INVOICE

INVOICE NO.	3
DATE/TAX POINT	*
ACCOUNT REF.	003

QUANTITY	DETAILS	DISC	NET PRICE	VAT
2	Datasaver env.	0.00	208.04	35.68
3	Diskbox $3^1/2$	0.00	29.85	5.12
... AS INVOICED ...			***NET***	237.89
			VAT	40.80
			TOTAL	278.69

Paperbox Express Ltd
Braebank Mill
Inverkip Road
Greenock
PA16 8FT

Tel: 01475 33446
Fax: 01475 36778

VAT No: 220 5564 12

Giftbox Ltd
76 Queensway
Redhill
Surrey
RH1 3WE

INVOICE

INVOICE NO.	4
DATE/TAX POINT	*
ACCOUNT REF.	004

QUANTITY	DETAILS	DISCOUNT	NET PRICE	VAT
2	Labels 127 × 49	0.00	167.40	28.71
2	Printout binder	0.00	105.20	18.04
... AS INVOICED ...			*NET*	272.60
			VAT	46.75
			TOTAL	319.35

Paperbox Express Ltd
Braebank Mill
Inverkip Road
Greenock
PA16 8FT

Tel: 01475 33446
Fax: 01475 36778

VAT No: 220 5564 12

Denton Stationery Suppliers
87 Crown Street
Guide Bridge
Manchester
M23 4EF

INVOICE

INVOICE NO.	5
DATE/TAX POINT	*
ACCOUNT REF.	005

QUANTITY	DETAILS	DISC	NET PRICE	VAT
1	Labels 89 × 49	0.00	71.20	12.21
3	Labels 127 × 49	0.00	251.10	43.06
3	Printout binder	0.00	157.80	27.06
1	Printout binder	0.00	52.60	9.02

... AS INVOICED ...

NET	532.70
VAT	91.35
TOTAL	624.05

STATEMENT	REMITTANCE ADVICE

Paper Box Express Ltd
Braebank Mill
Invertrip Road
Greenock

A/C ref	000001
Date	*
Page	1

Abraham & Matthews Ltd
152 High Street
Romford
Essex
RM1 1JU

Date	Ref	Details	Debit	Credit
*	1	Expanding discbox		
*	1	Multibox 5¼		
*	1	Labels 102 × 49	815.25	

Current	30 Day	60 Day	90 Day	120+ Day
815.25				

Amount due 815.25

Paper Box Express Ltd
Braebank Mill
Invertrip Road
Greenock

A/C ref	000001
Date	*
Page	1

Abraham & Matthews Ltd
152 High Street
Romford
Essex
RM1 1JU

Date	Ref	Details	Debit	Credit
*	1	Expanding diskcbox		
*	1	Multibox 5¼		
*	1	Labels 102 × 49		815.25

Amount due 815.25

Sales Ledger Account Balances (Aged)

A/C	Account Name	Turnover	Credit limit	Balance	Current	30 Days	60 Days	90 Days	Other
1	Abraham & Matthews	815.25	1,000	815.25	815.25				
2	Qwerty Office Supplies	162.12	1,000	162.12	162.12				
3	Ronald Earl Group	278.69	1,000	278.69	278.69				
4	Giftbox Ltd	319.35	1,000	319.35	319.35				
5	Denton Stationery	624.06	1,000	624.06	624.06				
	Totals	2,199.47	5,000	2,199.47	2,199.47				

Purchase Ledger Account Balances (Aged)

A/C	Account Name	Turnover	Credit limit	Balance	Current	30 Days	60 Days	90 Days	Other
1	First Class Suppliers	405.12	3,000	405.12	405.12				
2	Davidson Stationers Ltd	275.60	3,000	275.60	275.60				
3	Computerise Ltd	145.57	3,000	145.57	145.57				
4	Paper Products Ltd	3,511.95	3,000	3,511.95	3,511.95				
5	Plastics Unlimited	523.65	3,000	523.65	523.65				
	Totals	4,861.89	15,000	4,861.89	4,861.89				

Note: Not all programs produce an aged creditors report.

ASSIGNMENT 3: JP HARTNELL LTD

GLYNNS & WILLIAMS BANK PLC
5 Main Road, Solihull

99 - 88 - 77

7th April 19 *95*

Pay *Trevor Partridge* or order

One Hundred and Sixty Two Pounds £ 162.96

96 Pence ******************

JP Hartnell Ltd

000070 99 - 88 - 77 4465879944

PAYSLIP

		RATE	GROSS PAY	DEDUCTIONS		CUMULATIVES	
Hourly basic:	38.0000	4.6700	177.46	PAYE Tax	32.92	Total gross pay TD	212.49
Overtime:	5.0000	7.0050	35.03	National Ins.	16.61	Gross for tax TD	212.49
	-	-	-	Pension	-	Tax paid TD	32.92
	-	-	-		-	Earnings for NI TD	212.00
	-	-	-		-	National Ins. TD	16.61
	-	-	-		-	Pension TD	-
					-		
Sick pay	-	-	-		-	Earnings for NI	212.00
Maternity pay	-	-	-	Rounding b/f	-	Gross for tax	212.49
Holiday pay	-	-	-	Rounding c/f	-	TOTAL GROSS PAY	212.49
						National Ins Number	HJ452312J

1	07/04/95	1	CW	352L	3	TREVOR PARTRIDGE	Net pay
Week	Date	Dept	Payment	Tax code	Employee ref		£162.96

GLYNNS & WILLIAMS BANK PLC **99 - 88 - 77**
5 Main Road, Solihull

28th April 19 95

Pay *Andrew Kershaw* or order

Seven Hundred and Forty One Pounds £ 741.19

19 Pence ******************

JP Hartnell Ltd

000071 99 - 88 - 77 4465879944

PAYSLIP

		RATE	GROSS PAY	DEDUCTIONS		CUMULATIVES	
Monthly basic:	1.0000	750.00	750.00	PAYE Tax	215.16	Total gross pay TD	1039.99
	-	-	-	National Ins.	83.64	Gross for tax TD	1039.99
	-	-	-	Pension	-	Tax paid TD	215.16
Commission:	-	-	289.99		-	Earnings for NI TD	1036.00
	-	-	-		-	National Ins. TD	83.64
	-	-	-		-	Pension TD	-
					-		
Sick pay	-	-	-		-	Earnings for NI	1036.00
Maternity pay	-	-	-	Rounding b/f	-	Gross for tax	1039.99
Holiday pay	-	-	-	Rounding c/f	-	TOTAL GROSS PAY	1039.99
						National Ins Number	LK348755K

1	28/04/95	2	QM	150T	4	ANDREW KERSHAW	Net pay
Month	Date	Dept	Payment	Tax code	Employee ref		£741.19

JP HARTNELL
PAYMENTS SUMMARY – PART 1
Weekly

Date: 07/04/95
Page: 1

Ref.	Total gross pay	Taxable gross pay	Pre-tax Addition	Pre-tax Deduct'n	Pension	PAYE	Nat. Ins.	SSP	SMP	Post-Tax Addition	Post-Tax Deduct'n	Amount B/F	Amount C/F	Net pay
1	212.49	212.49	0.00	0.00	0.00	32.92	16.61	0.00	0.00	0.00	0.00	0.00	0.00	162.96
1 employee	212.49	212.49	0.00	0.00	0.00	32.92	16.61	0.00	0.00	0.00	0.00	0.00	0.00	162.96

PAYMENTS SUMMARY – PART 2
National Insurance

Ref.	Name	Standard earnings	Total contribution	Employees contribution	Con/out earnings	Con/Out contribution	Employers Nat. Ins.	Employers Pension	Tax code	Nat. Ins. category
1	T Partridge	212.00	38.28	16.61	0.00	0.00	21.67	0.00	352L	A
Total values for 1 employee		212.00	38.28	16.61	0.00	0.00	21.67	0.00		

PAYMENTS SUMMARY – PART 3
Year to date

Ref.	Name	Total gross pay	Taxable gross pay	PAYE	National Insurance Employees	National Insurance Employers	SSP	SMP	Pension Employee	Pension Employer
1	T Partridge	212.49	212.49	32.92	16.61	21.67	0.00	0.00	0.00	0.00
Total values for 1 employee		212.49	212.49	32.92	16.61	21.67	0.00	0.00	0.00	0.00

JP HARTNELL
PAYMENTS SUMMARY – PART 1
Monthly

Date: 28/04/95
Page: 1

Ref.	Total gross pay	Taxable gross pay	Pre-tax Addition	Pre-tax Deduct'n	Pension	PAYE	Nat. Ins.	SSP	SMP	Post-Tax Addition	Post-Tax Deduct'n	Amount B/F	Amount C/F	Net pay
2	1039.99	1039.99	289.99	0.00	0.00	215.16	83.64	0.00	0.00	0.00	0.00	0.00	0.00	741.19
1 employee	1039.99	1039.99	289.99	0.00	0.00	215.16	83.64	0.00	0.00	0.00	0.00	0.00	0.00	741.19

PAYMENTS SUMMARY – PART 2
National Insurance

Ref.	Name	Standard earnings	Total contribution	Employees contribution	Con/out earnings	Con/Out contribution	Employers Nat. Ins.	Employers Pension	Tax code	Nat. Ins. category
2	A Kershaw	1036.00	189.52	83.64	0.00	0.00	105.88	0.00	150T	A
Total values for 1 employee		1036.00	189.52	83.64	0.00	0.00	105.88	0.00		

PAYMENTS SUMMARY – PART 3
Year to date

Ref.	Name	Total gross pay	Taxable gross pay	PAYE	National Insurance Employees	National Insurance Employers	SSP	SMP	Pension Employee	Pension Employer
2	A Kershaw	1036.99	1039.99	215.16	83.64	105.88	0.00	0.00	0.00	0.00
Total values for 1 employee		1036.99	1039.99	215.16	83.64	105.88	0.00	0.00	0.00	0.00

EMPLOYER'S PAYMENT RECORD (FORM P32)

Date: 28/04/95

(1) Total SSP	*(2) SSP recovered*	*(3) SMP*	*(4) NIC comp'n*	*(5) Total ded.*	*(6) Gross NI*	*(7) Net NI*	*(8) PAYE tax*	*(9) Total due*
0.00	0.00	0.00	0.00	0.00	227.80	227.80	248.08	475.88

NIC compensation percentage	*Employee range*	*Date range*
SMP: 0.00	0001–0005	Week: 06/04/95–31/05/95 Month: 06/04/95–05/05/95

Simulations

SIMULATION (UNITS 1, 2 AND 20): NATURAL PRODUCTS LTD

Element 1 Input information from source documents into a computer system

- All vital fields are completed

  Incomplete or unauthorised source documents are referred for clarification

- All errors in inputting and coding are identified and corrected
- Correct part of the computer system is used for inputting
- New unique reference codes are generated as necessary
- Inputting is completed to agreed deadline

  Organisational procedures for filing source documents are followed

- Risks to the information technology environment are minimised at all times

Range

Information

- words
- numbers
- information to be coded

Source documents

- complete
- incomplete

Computer systems

- databases
  spreadsheets

Types of inputting

- addition of new info
  modification of existing info
  deletion/cancellation

Databases

stock control
- customers
- sales ledgers
- purchase ledgers

employees
cash logs

Unique reference numbers

- stock codes
- customer references
- invoice numbers

employee numbers

Element 3 Generate and print standard reports on a computer system

- Required range and report correctly specified
- Printed information is correct and complete
- Hard copy is clean, clearly printed and aligned correctly
- Efforts are made to minimise the wastage of paper
- Printer area is kept clean and tidy
- Work is produced to agreed deadline
- Documents are correctly collated and distributed as directed
- Risks to the information technology environment are minimised at all times

Range

Generation

- specification of start and finish
- selection of required report

Standard reports

bar charts
pie charts
histograms
- standard database reports

Computer systems

- databases

spreadsheets

Standard database reports

- invoices
  payments
  pay runs
- statements of account
  infringement reports
  flexitime reports

FACTFILE

Business name	Natural Products Ltd	
Location	Taunton, Somerset	
Personnel	Managing director	Cindy Taylor
	Sales director	Jason Taylor
	Production director	Tracy Yard
	Financial director	Steve Roberts
Address	151 Green Lane Taunton TA20 6GH	
Telephone	01823 452211	
Fax	01823 348899	
VAT Reg. No.	322 5833 23	
Number of accounts	20 of each	
Last invoice no.	5445	
Business	Manufacture, wholesale and mail order sale of toiletries and cosmetics	

Business profile

The business was started in 1978 by Cindy Taylor. Early success in supplying natural products to a famous retail chain led to Cindy's husband, Jason, and brother-in-law, Steve, joining the company.

The company originally based its business on products marketed under the customer's own label. Major customers continue to be supermarket and drugstore chains.

Sales increased steadily throughout the 1980s. In 1989, encouraged by her own staff, Cindy launched a new range of products marketed under the company's own name. These products are only available by mail order. A catalogue is produced annually.

The company hopes to be floated on the stock market soon, although the directors appreciate certain improvements will be required first in the accounting systems.

The company specialises in products which use as many natural ingredients as possible. The directors are leading campaigners against animal testing.

Accounts department

Accounts supervisor	Caroline Everley
Ledger clerk	You
Administration and payroll	Robert Foster
Cashier and petty cashier	Trudi Roberts

Terms of trade

The company is registered for VAT. All sales are standard-rated.

All wholesale customers are allowed settlement discounts of 2% if invoices are paid within 14 days of the date of the invoice and all customers have a credit limit of £3,500.

Certain suppliers offer settlement discounts.

System changeover

The company has decided to change over to a new computerised system. As part of this changeover it has decided to analyse sales in a more complex way.

Sales procedures

All sales are despatched from the main warehouse. Sales invoices are raised from *despatch listings*. The company has an integrated debtors' ledger and nominal ledger system.

Credit notes are raised from *returns listings*.

Mail order receipts and sales in the staff shop are input through a sales invoice.

Purchasing procedures

All purchases are made by two purchasers who work within the production department. The purchasers maintain *masterfiles* of supplier details and pricelists.

Letters of enquiry are sent to various suppliers requesting *quotations* for the supply of specific goods. The quotations are then compared and an official *purchase order* is sent. (The production director approves all purchase orders.)

The administration assistant checks and processes all *purchase invoices*. The ledger clerk makes the postings to the creditors' and nominal ledgers (from batch headers) and deals with all queries.

Credit notes are included on purchase order batch headers as *negative amounts*.

YOUR ASSIGNMENT

Setting up files

1 This is the first day of the new accounting year and the first day of the changeover.

Record all the opening balances using the current run date. Perform the month-end procedures to re-set the ageing, etc.

Set up stock categories and product codes, and enter opening quantities.

2 Leave the system then re-enter. Set the run-date to one month later. (This makes the assumption that the opening balances in the debtors' and creditors' ledgers are unpaid amounts from the previous month only.)

If your package does not allow this function, use the current run date, but the ageing on your reports will be different from the solution. NP Ltd does not wish to produce stock value reports so you do not need to input unit costs into the stock system.

Processing transactions

1 Raise sales invoices for the latest batch of despatches. The next invoice number is 5446.
2 Raise sales credit notes for the latest batch of returns.
3 Post purchase invoices and credit notes received from the batch header.
4 Record cash receipts and payments from the cash book.
5 Write off sales invoice no. 5330 as a bad debt.

Printing out reports

1 Print out statements of account to send to customers.
2 Print out the aged purchase ledger listing and the aged sales ledger listing.
3 Print out the trial balance (nominal ledger listing) and the VAT return analysis.

Customers

Code		*Invoice No.*	*Net* £	*VAT* £	*Gross* £
1	Dehlavi Kosmetayos	5330	345.67	59.28	404.95
	388 Commercial Road	5439	234.45	40.21	274.66
	Bristol				
	BS1 3UH				
	Richard Allen				
2	Cosmetic Co Ltd	5331	123.45	21.17	144.62
	234 Grange Road	5334	23.44	4.02	27.46
	Twickenham	5345	1,564.66	268.34	1,833.00
	TW23 5TR				
	Lawrence Deardon				
3	Mexican Products Ltd	5333	455.67	78.15	533.82
	356 Union Street	5340	177.88	30.51	208.39
	London				
	N14 5TH				
4	Green & Green Ltd	5339	567.45	97.32	664.77
	356 Royal Way	5443	23.56	4.04	27.60
	Chelmsford				
	Essex				
	CM2 6FG				
	Chris Bailey				

Code		*Invoice No.*	*Net* £	*VAT* £	*Gross* £
5	Health Promotions Ltd 289 Park Road North Newcastle NE13 5RD Bob Rimmer	5335	876.56	150.33	1,026.89
6	Mail order and staff sales				

Suppliers

Code		*Invoice No.*	*Net* £	*VAT* £	*Gross* £
1	Adler Electrical Supplies 223 Blackwood Road St Albans AL1 1SA Fred Smith	23445 23447	677.45 134.66	118.55 23.57	796.00 158.23
2	Blackwood Foodstuffs & Additives Ltd 244 Parker Street Leatherhead KT22 8AG Peter Forrest	23449 23488	187.56 344.70	32.49 59.72	220.05 404.42
3	Arthur Chong Ltd 233 Leigh Street Leeds LS21 4YH Lee Chong	23455 23481	366.46 845.66	64.13 147.99	430.59 993.65
4	English Gas plc South West House 12 Bennetts Court Bristol BS12 3WE Business users dept	23457	768.45		768.45
5	Green Chemical Co Ltd Imperial Avenue Nottingham NG24 4RE Stuart Frost	23466 23480	270.05 47.44	46.31 8.14	316.36 55.58

Nominal codes and opening trial balance income

Income

4000	Sales: Type A, B, C and D – Shampoo and conditioner	
4001	Sales: Type A, B, C and D – Bath products	
4002	Sales: Type A, B, C and D – Soap	
4100	Sales: Type A, B, C and D – Baby products	
4101	Sales: Type A, B, C and D – Cosmetics	
4904	Rent income	
5009	Discounts taken	

Purchases

5000	Materials purchases	

Expenditure

4009	Discounts allowed	
7003	Staff salaries	
7100	Rent	
7201	Gas	
7502	Telephone	
7501	Postage and carriage	
7504	Stationery	
7400	Travel and subsistence	
8204	General insurance	
7800	Repairs and renewals	
7803	Building expenses (misc.)	
7304	Miscellaneous motor expenses	
6900	Miscellaneous expenses	
8205	Refreshments	
7801	Cleaning	
8100	Bad debts write-off	
7900	Bank interest paid	
7903	Loan interest paid	

Assets

0010	Fixed assets – Freehold property	150,779.50
0020	Fixed assets – Plant and machinery	167,345.67
0040	Fixed assets – Fixtures and fittings	45,234.67
1001	Stock	25,789.45
1100	Debtors control account	5,146.16
1200	Bank (current account)	12,345.45
1210	Cash at bank (deposit account)	250,000.00
1230	Petty cash	200.00

Liabilities

2100	Creditors control account	4,143.33
2310	Hire purchase	10,786.45
2200	Control account (current VAT)	Nil
2201	Tax VAT balance b/f	25,564.33

Capital and reserves

3000	Ordinary shares	50,000.00
3100	Reserves	15,875.00
3200	Profit and loss account	550,471.90

Product listing
Wholesale price list and units in stock

		£ *(excl. VAT) each*	*Quantity*
Shampoo and conditioner			
1	Lavender shampoo	2.49	0
2	Travel wash	1.49	0
3	Coconut grove	2.49	40
4	Untangled	1.49	40
5	Egg whip	1.49	20
Bath products			
6	Raspberry treat	1.49	0
7	Lemon treat	1.49	20
8	Pretty bubbles	1.99	40
9	Passionfruit	2.49	40
Soap			
10	Soapy Molloy	0.99	20
11	Sand rub	1.99	25
12	Fruit fool	1.49	6
Baby products			
13	Baby bubbles	1.49	0
14	Baby soap	0.99	15
15	Baby shampoo	1.49	6
Cosmetics			
16	Day	9.49	30
17	Evening	9.49	30
18	Summer	5.49	0
19	Spring	5.49	20
20	Autumn	5.49	0

DESPATCH LISTING

Batch No. 345
Date *

Customer	*Account No.*	*Product*	*Quantity*
Cosmetic Company Ltd	2	5	10
		10	20
Health Promotions Ltd	5	4	30
		7	10
		9	40
Dehlavi Kosmetayos	1	11	15
		14	10
		19	10
Mexican Products Ltd	3	8	20
		17	20
Cosmetic Company Ltd	2	3	30
		16	20

RETURNS LISTING

Batch No. 346
Date *

RN No.	*Customer*	*Account No.*	*Product*	*Quantity*	*Reason for credit*
122	Green & Green Ltd	4	5	5	Damaged
123	Health Promotions Ltd	5	6	10	Overdelivery

BATCH HEADER

Invoice No.	*Supplier*	*Nominal code*	*Net*	*VAT £*	*Total £*
23490	Adler Electrical Supplies	7800	23.56	4.12	27.68
23491	Blackwood Foodstuffs	5000	422.10	73.13	495.23
23492	Green Chemical Co.	5000	556.45	95.43	651.88
23493	Arthur Chong Ltd	5000	755.02	132.13	887.15
23494	Green Chemical Co.	5000	344.23	59.04	403.27

STAFF & MAIL ORDER SALES SUMMARY

Return No. 1
Date *

Category of sale	*Nominal code*	*Net*	*VAT* £	*Total* £
Shampoo and conditioner	4000	223.56		
Bath products	4001	156.77		
Soap	4002	133.44		
Baby products	4100	244.03		
Cosmetics	4101	87.56		
Totals		845.36	147.93	993.29

CASH BOOK RECEIPTS

Date	Narrative	Invoices paid	Total £	Debtors £	Rent £	Other £	VAT £	Discount £
*	Mexican Products Ltd	5333	524.71	524.71				9.11
*	Green & Green Ltd	5339	644.84	644.84				11.20
*	Cosmetic Company	Unknown	1,026.89	1,026.89				
*	Transfer (deposit account)		10,000.00			10,000.00		
*	Mail order and staff sales		993.29	993.29				
*	Freeman & Jenkins		600.00		600.00			
	Totals		13,789.73	3,189.73	600.00	10,000.00		20.31

CASH BOOK PAYMENTS

Date	Narrative	Cheque no.	Invoices paid	Total £	Debtors £	Rent £	Other £	VAT £	Discount £
*	Alder Electrical Supplies	655	23445 23447	954.23	954.23				
*	Arthur Chong Ltd	656	23455	310.88	310.88				
*	Green Chemical Co.	657	23466	310.96	310.96				5.40
*	Kingsbury Insurance	DD		123.66			123.66		
*	Monthly salaries	CT		16,345.39			16,345.66		
	Totals			18,045.39	1,576.07		16,469.32		5.40

SIMULATION (UNITS 3 AND 20): TOP TRAVEL LTD

Element 1 Input information from source documents into a computer system

- All vital fields are completed
- Incomplete or unauthorised source documents are referred for clarification
- All errors in inputting and coding are identified and corrected
- Correct part of the computer system is used for inputting
- New unique reference codes are generated as necessary
- Inputting is completed to agreed deadline
- Organisational procedures for filing source documents are followed
- Risks to the information technology environment are minimised at all times

Range

Information

- words
- numbers
- information to be coded

Source documents

- complete
- incomplete

Computer systems

- databases
- spreadsheets

Types of inputting

- addition of new info
- modification of existing info
- deletion/cancellation

Databases

- stock control
- customers
- sales ledgers
- purchase ledgers
- employees
- cash logs

Unique reference numbers

- stock codes
- customer references
- invoice numbers
- employee numbers

Element 2 Locate and retrieve recorded details of requested items from a computer system

- Correct details are retrieved
- Search facilities are used optimally
- Confidential information is not disclosed to unauthorised people
- Risks to the information technology environments are minimised at all times

Range

Methods of requesting items

- specification of unique reference codes
- specification of details

Methods of locating details

- automatic searching
- manual searching (browsing)

Computer systems

- databases
- spreadsheets

Databases

- stock control
- customers
- sales ledgers
- purchase ledgers
- employees
- cash logs

Examples of recorded details of requested items

- cost codes
- type of payment of an order
- progress and status of an order
- credit limit/status/worthiness of an order
- employee details
- grant codes for courses

Element 3 Generate and print standard reports on a computer system

- Required range and report correctly specified
- Printed information is correct and complete
- Hard copy is clean, printed clearly and aligned correctly
- Efforts are made to minimise the wastage of paper
- Printer area is kept clean and tidy
- Work is produced to agreed deadlines
- Documents are correctly collated and distributed as directed
- Risks to the information technology environment are minimised at all times

Range

Generation

- specification of start and finish
- selection of required report

Standard reports

- bar charts
- pie charts
- histograms
- standard database reports

Computer systems

- databases
- spreadsheets

Standard database reports

- invoices
- payments
- pay runs
- statements of account
- infringement reports
- flexitime reports

FACTFILE

Business name	Top Travel Ltd	
Location	25 travel shops in UK Head office in Birmingham	
Bank details	Bristol Branch Southern Bank plc 20–11–91	
Tax office ref.	665/P1222	
Personnel	Managing director Finance director Sales director Personnel director	Jane Priestley Franz Muller Phillippa Edwards Colin Berriman
Business	Travel agents catering for the independent traveller, selling mostly international flights and European rail and ferry tickets.	

Pension scheme

Type of fund	COMP scheme
COMP ref.	MP665211
SCON ref.	S4/665555B
Name and address of fund	Surefire Life Insurance 151 Parkway Drive Withington Manchester M21 5TF
Telephone	0161 860 5588
Contact	Peter Thompson

Business profile

The business was founded fifteen years ago and has grown through the acquisition of small independent travel shops throughout the country.

Most of the staff in the shops have been employed on the basis of their experience of world travel, rather than previous selling experience.

Payroll procedures

All payroll is processed centrally and paid by Giro.

Employees' hours worked are recorded on timesheets which are authorised by each shop manager.

Certain employees are members of the company occupational pension scheme. Deductions made towards the scheme are paid over monthly by cheque.

You are responsible for preparing the payroll for one shop (Manchester). All employees are paid monthly.

YOUR ASSIGNMENT

Preparing monthly payroll

Existing employees

Set up files for the following employees.

Employee 1

Surname	Bradley	
First name	Peter	
Status	Single	
NI number	GH 34 28 66 K	
Tax code	500H	
Tax basis	Normal cumulative	
Birth date	13-4-62	
Join date	23-5-89	
Director	No	
Payment method	Giro	
Bank sort code	78-56-34	
Bank/branch	Southern/Bramhall	
Account number	98875677	
Rate of pay	£1,041.67	
NI letter	A (becoming D as from 06/03/96)	
Address	344 Langley Park Bramhall Stockport	
		£
b/f figures (months 1 to 11)	Total gross pay	11,586.54
	Total taxable pay	11,586.54
	Tax paid	1,601.83
National Insurance b/f	Letter	A
	Employee	924.44
	Employer	1,169.08
	Gross pay for NI	11,586
Pension fund member	Joining this month	
Contributions	Employee 3% Employer 4%	

Peter Bradley is to receive 6 hours overtime at £6.40 per hour. He has also decided to start contributing £3.00 a month to charity under the new company payroll giving scheme.

Employee 2

Surname	Pettigrew	
First name	Jane	
Title	Miss	
NI number	DE 23 98 55 L	
Tax code	352L	
Tax basis	Week 1/Month 1	
Birth date	20–7–68	
Join date	12–11–90	
Director	No	
Payment method	Giro	
Bank sort code	45–77–01	
Bank/branch	Northern/Eccles	
Account number	63302233	
Rate of pay	£708.33 per month	
NI letter	A	
Address	133 Castlebank Way Eccles Manchester	
b/f figures (months 1 to 11)	Total pay	7,952.08
	Total taxable pay	7,952.08
	Tax	1,032.58
National Insurance b/f	Letter	A
	Employee	306.79
	Employer	557.90
	Std NI earnings	7,952
Pension fund member	No	

Jane received a bonus of £500 at the year-end, ie. 31 March 1996.

Jane has also decided to start saving £10.00 a month under the company's SAYE scheme (which is linked to the employee share option scheme operated by the company).

New employee

You have already checked the P45 and are satisfied that the brought forward figures are correct.

Surname	Ferguson
First name	Karen
NI number	DF 23 45 88 H
Tax code	BR
Birth date	13–6–64
Join date	06/03/96
Director	No
Payment method	Giro
Bank sort code	55–87–45
Bank/branch	Midwestern/Stockport
Account number	34552233
Rate of pay	£800 per month
NI letter	A
Address	223 Cherry Tree Lane Stockport

b/f figures (months 1 to 11)	Total pay	7,000.00
	Total taxable pay	7,000.00
	Tax	1,750.00

Pension fund member No

Processing monthly payroll

Run the monthly payroll for month 12.

Print out the following reports:

- payslips;
- BACS/Giro listing;
- payroll summary;
- PAYE remittance report.

Run the month-end closure procedure. (You may have to run this *before* running certain reports.)

Year-end returns

Print out the following reports:

- P35; and
- P14/60.

Index

Publications Questionnaire

FTC

At Financial Training we are interested in knowing your views of our products. We would appreciate your assistance in helping us to maintain our high standards by completing this simple questionnaire.

1 Title of publication ______________________________

2 Content

For each question, tick the box which most closely reflects your view.

	Excellent	Good	Satisfactory	Poor
Did the content cover the syllabus thoroughly?	☐	☐	☐	☐
Was the writing style clear and easy to understand?	☐	☐	☐	☐
Were the worked examples useful and relevant?	☐	☐	☐	☐
Were there sufficient diagrams, graphs and tables?	☐	☐	☐	☐
Were the exam style questions beneficial?	☐	☐	☐	☐
Were the answers to questions comprehensive?	☐	☐	☐	☐
Were the style and layout clear?	☐	☐	☐	☐

3 General

Please suggest any improvements that you feel would be beneficial:

____

____

____

Have you noticed any errors in this publication? If so, please specify?

Page **Error**

______ ______________________________

______ ______________________________

______ ______________________________

4 Further information

If you would like to receive information on other Financial Training products and courses, please supply your name and address:

____

____

Thank you for your co-operation.

Please return your completed questionnaire to:

Production Department
Financial Training
136–142 Bramley Road, London W10 6SR